FARROW&BALL

THE ART OF COLOR

FARROW&BALL
THE ART OF COLOR

BRIAN D. COLEMAN
PHOTOGRAPHS BY EDWARD ADDEO

Gibbs Smith, Publisher
TO ENRICH AND INSPIRE HUMANKIND

Salt Lake City | Charleston | Santa Fe | Santa Barbara

First Edition

15 14 13   10 9 8

Published by
Gibbs Smith, Publisher
P.O. Box 667
Layton, Utah 84041

Orders: 1.800.835.4993
www.gibbs-smith.com

Designed by Debra McQuiston
Printed and bound in China
Engraving Artwork by EclectiCollection™

Library of Congress Cataloging-in-Publication Data

Coleman, Brian D.
  Farrow and Ball : the art of color / Brian Coleman ; photographs by Edward
Addeo. -- 1st ed.
      p. cm.
  ISBN-13: 978-1-4236-0010-7
  ISBN-10: 1-4236-0010-X
  1. Color in interior decoration--United States. 2. Color decoration and
ornament--United States. 3. Paint. 4. Farrow & Ball. I. Title.
  NK2115.5.C6C65 2007
  747'.94--dc22
                        2006102871

To R.S., my Sayang, who helps me relax. —B.C.

To Ruth, my wife, whose gifts and talents are an inspiration to me.

To Julia, my daughter, whose dedication to music is a constant reminder of the discipline and rigor necessary to keep your passion alive.

To Willie, my best friend, who lowers my blood pressure and makes me smile. —E.A.

Contents

PREFACE

IN AN AGE when manufacturers seem to think that in order to be commercially viable every product has to be labeled "state of the art," "cutting edge" or at the very least "new," the English paint company Farrow & Ball has become very successful, indeed, by rediscovering the past.

Farrow & Ball was founded in the 1930s by chemists John Farrow and Richard Ball. They set up business in Dorset, the county of that quintessential English writer Thomas Hardy, in the ancient town of Wimborne. There they made limewash, distemper and dead-flat oil paints, selling these products to a select band of country-house customers. The company continued along, unchanged, until the early 1990s, when it came into the hands of Tom Helme and Martin Ephson, who saw in it a potential undreamed of by its founders.

In 1990 Tom was working on a restoration project for the National Trust at an important eighteenth-century country house in Devon. He had been trying to duplicate a paint color, making up test pots, mixing colors, even making paint from scratch using dry pigment, but with little success. One day a decorator from a local firm turned up with some tins of Farrow & Ball paints, and to Tom's amazement, there was the color that he had been working so hard to come up with, ready-made . Tom went to Wimborne, where he found a company that was, in his words, "operating in something of a time warp," but which, nonetheless, was making high-quality products of a type Tom had thought unavailable commercially. Tom had stumbled on what he called an "undiscovered gem," and he went back to the National Trust with the news that there was a paint manufacturer in Dorset that would make any color a restoration job might require.

The National Trust was so impressed that they joined forces with Farrow & Ball to launch a jointly branded range of paints. What they came up with soon found favor with decorators and a public anxious to get their hands on traditional, high-quality paints in time-honored colors that worked together.

Enter the other man in this story, Martin Ephson. Martin and Tom had been friends since schooldays. Tom told his friend about Farrow & Ball and in so doing also communicated the enthusiasm he felt for the company. Martin's background in corporate finance had taught him not to let personal feelings get in the way of economic reality, but after looking at the company closely, he became convinced that there was an opportunity to take it forward. Together they joined Farrow & Ball in 1992 and eventually, with the owner of the company going into retirement, were in a position to buy it.

They immediately set about putting their acquisition on a modern business footing. The product was made available to a wider audience while the integrity of its manufacturing methods was carefully preserved. The company's product turnover began to climb, and with this came the confidence to launch the highly successful range of "Archive" paints in 1994. In that same year, Farrow& Ball's first independent stockist was appointed, and the following year the manufacture of wallpaper was transferred from Norfolk to the site in Wimborne. And all the while, Tom and Martin ensured that their new company remained true to its past of producing traditional top-quality paint.

Colors were chosen from the best of the past and were based on historical examples that generations of decorators and owners had used, knowing them to be successful. Today, these tried and tested colors have found their place in every kind of interior the twenty-first century has to offer, from country houses to loft conversions and everything in between. In fact, this eclectic mix of customers accounts for the company's ability to thrive and prosper in the world of big paint manufacturers. In 1992, Farrow & Ball was selling a million dollars worth of product a year; now the company does that in a week. They export to thirty-three countries on five continents and in 2004 won the Queen's Award for Export Achievement. In 2002, Farrow & Ball opened its first showroom in the United States in New York. Two years later, a second showroom followed in Beverly Hills, and others later followed in Chicago, Boston, Washington. D.C., and Greenwich, whilst in 2006 Farrow

& Ball was listed as one of the United States' thirty most influential home brands in the much-respected Robb Report.

At the time of this writing, Farrow & Ball is undergoing some changes in management. Tom Helme and Martin Ephson decided to retire and the company is now run by a management team drawn from Farrow & Ball's loyal staff, those who worked alongside the two men who managed to turn an "undiscovered gem" into a company that has taken its place on the world's stage. As for Farrow & Ball's paints and wallpapers, nothing has changed; they remain what they have always been—bywords for tradition, quality and classic taste.

INTRODUCTION

ONE OF THE MOST important parts in successful design is applying the right color and finish of paint. The richly saturated colors of Farrow & Ball, one of the leading manufacturers of specialty paints and wallpapers, has been quietly gaining recognition in the United States and Canada. Located in southwest England in the picturesque Dorset countryside, the company has been in business for more than fifty years, producing traditionally made paints for clients ranging from the National Trust to the Royal Navy.

In this book, the first ever published on the use of Farrow & Ball products in North America, we travel across the continent from Miami to Maine, Canada to California visiting a wide selection of extraordinary and inspired interiors. From a Manhattan designer's classically furnished pre-war apartment in New York City to a university professor's post-modern glass and concrete home in Toronto, we see how Farrow & Ball colors are used. Homes range from a colorful cottage on a picturesque island off the coast of Maine—decorated in Farrow & Ball Yankee colors of "Dorset Cream," with indigo blue "Tented Stripe" wallpaper and "Rectory Red" painted floors—to a traditionally elegant, historic brick mansion in Richmond, Virginia—restored with a muted Farrow & Ball palette of warm, neutral "Pointing" (named after the color of lime pointing used in brickwork) with chalky, stone-colored "Clunch" and tranquil "Green Blue" accents. A special treat is a glimpse into the spectacular England estates of the two owners of the company, Martin Ephson and Thomas Helme, who use Farrow & Ball paints and papers in traditional English settings.

Farrow & Ball paints contain 32 percent more pigment than the industry standard, giving them an unusual depth and resulting in richer, more saturated colors. All paints are mixed on-site and a state-of-the-art quality control lab at the factory ensures that formulas are consistent and color variation is not visible to the human eye. Not sold locally (one can't buy a gallon or two of "Bible

Black" or "Eating Room Red" at the local hardware store), Farrow & Ball paint is available only from the Dorset factory and carefully selected independent showrooms. Three-ounce sample pots are provided for customers to test at home and then place their order, which is shipped directly from England; the color and consistency of each paint color is guaranteed to match exactly that in the sample pots. The company now produces 132 historically inspired colors ranging from "Mouse's Back." a quiet, neutral dark stone or drab found in early-eighteenth-century interiors, to "Ointment Pink," an early-nineteenth-

century color based on scrapings from the dining room at historic Calke Abbey.

Farrow & Ball also produces traditionally inspired wallpapers that are printed using water-based paints rather than modern inks, making thicker, more textured papers with a chalky, less shiny finish. Stripes are one of the specialties—there are seventy-two patterns from which to choose. Striped papers are printed using the nineteenth-century pan method, where the paper is slowly passed under troughs containing paint that filters onto bristles, creating a dragged or striped effect. Patterned papers are made with traditional eighteenth-century flatbed block printing as paint is applied to blocks and then gently pressed onto the ground paper.

Wallpaper patterns are simple—just two colors—with a variety of colorways for easier selection. They range from "St. Antoine's," an eighteenth-century design based on a 1793 damask paper, to "Sweet Pea," a classic Edwardian paper found in an early-twentieth-century home in England.

Color properly chosen and applied is the foundation for any good design. It is my hope that by celebrating Farrow & Ball paints and papers, this book will be an inspiration for designers, homeowners and everyone who appreciates the importance of the role of color in interior design.

The dining room
mantel glows with the magic of
the Emerald City of Oz.
Magnified by "Cooking Apple
Green" walls, the light flickers
in the large chemist's vials filled
with green water. Antique
English creamware is accented
by the "Lime White" mantel.

Barry Dixon
Fairy-tale Magic in Virginia

BARRY DIXON'S work and product line are regularly featured in publications and showrooms around the country. He likes to emphasize the importance of tradition, of creating interiors with a timeless appeal in which architecture is the foundation for good design. Color is his passion and the weaving of complementary hues in subtle harmonies one of his hallmarks. Brought up around the globe, Barry was raised on classic children's books that continue to influence his work today, often giving his interiors a fairy-tale charm and magic. And it is Barry's ability to bring the past into the present in unexpected and invigorating ways that makes his interiors unique and so popular. His own estate, Elway Hall in the rolling hills outside of Warrenton, Virginia, is one of the best testimonies to his design expertise.

Built in 1907 by a wealthy nineteenth-century industrialist for his daughter and son-in-law, General and Mrs. Spilman, the Edwardian mansion was the largest private residence in the area at the time. Constructed of native stones hauled to the site by oxen, it featured thirty-inch-thick walls, fourteen-foot ceilings, Tiffany stained and leaded glass windows, seventeen fireplaces and a grand carved oak staircase in the entry hall. Designed for entertaining, it remained the center of Warrenton social life for

The original oak staircase sweeps majestically downstairs to the main entry hall, which is made less imposing with walls painted in straightforward "Lime White."

more than fifty years. However, by the time Barry and his partner, Michael Schmidt, purchased it in 1999, the once-grand 20,000-square-foot home had been "updated" with period-inappropriate additions such as modern baths with built-in Jacuzzis and a contemporary black and white kitchen completely out of keeping with the historic character of the home.

Their main task was removing the renovations and returning the house to its original beauty while keeping it livable. Barry was careful not to change the layout of the home (original blueprints were, fortunately, still available), although he updated the rooms for the functions of contemporary life: the great hall became a more intimate sitting room; the original dining room was made into a family den; a smaller dining room was created out of an adjoining area; and a service room for servants was reborn as a breakfast nook. The generously scaled bedrooms were left untouched, although smaller, attached "guest" bedrooms meant for traveling servants were converted into children's rooms for visiting nieces and nephews. Electrical systems were updated, three new furnaces were added while carefully keeping the radiators intact, and the third-floor

THE GREAT HALL IS MADE INTO A MORE INTIMATE

sitting room by hanging sheer linen panels to divide it from the entry hall. Walls and plasterwork are painted a simple "Lime White" and the room is furnished with an eclectic collection of antiques, left. ❦ The chalky walls in the sitting room complement an eclectic assortment of antiques, including a goatskin cabinet and a plaster bust of a philosopher, above.

Vaseline-green orbs
and compotes rest on the
Steinway piano. The Tiffany
stained glass window is original,
its colors complemented
by the "Ciara Yellow" walls.

The former music room was made into a sun-filled garden room by painting the walls bright Irish *"Ciara Yellow"* and highlighting the ornate plasterwork with *"New White"* for an effect of Wedgwood Jasperware.

servants' quarters were converted into offices for Barry's design business.

Color was paramount in the restoration. Barry relied on the Farrow & Ball muted and chalky palette to help re-create the desired ambience of General Spilman's early-twentieth-century manor. Walls were painted "Lime White" in the large entry hall to highlight the original oak woodwork, and Barry added gossamer veils of sheer fabric to cloister the space and make it more intimate without damaging the original plaster walls. The main sitting room, originally the great hall, was softened and made more inviting with the addition of unlined linen panels that float across the room. The walls, saturated with "Lime White," alternately glisten with the summer sun and glow of firelight from the fireplace that is

kept burning all year round. Ornate plasterwork on the ceiling was kept intact and painted "Lime White" as well. The former music room was made into a sun-filled garden room by painting the walls bright Irish "Ciara Yellow" and highlighting the ornate plasterwork with "New White" for an effect of Wedgwood Jasperware. The formality of the room was deconstructed, with organic pieces, including an armillary once owned by Jacques Grange, set on a tall marble pedestal, massive stone spheres clustered on the floor and luminescent, nineteenth-century orbs of Waterford crystal placed atop the Steinway piano. Now one of Barry's favorite spots for reading, the room glows with magical color and light.

The dining room was made more intimate by painting its walls "Cooking Apple Green," while the mantel was painted "Lime White" and crowded with antique English creamware. Nineteenth-century glass chemist's

vials were filled with sparkling green water and placed on the mantel. Like large vats of absinthe, they reflect the flickering firelight, making the room dreamlike, a fairy-tale Emerald City in Virginia.

"Old White" was continued in the wide upstairs halls. Inspired by the Italian engravings of Claude Lorraine, the master suite was painted with a sepia-toned mural of views of the surrounding countryside—the vista if the walls had fallen away. Farrow & Ball colors were used throughout the design: "Dead Salmon," "Smoked Trout," "New White" and "Lime White." Sheers were strung around the curved walls of the tower at one end of the room, making an ethereal, floating retreat for the bed.

Other bedrooms include a red and white guest room painted in "All

Wedgwood's strongly colored Jasperware is the inspiration for the bright Irish
"Ciara Yellow" walls and ceiling in the music room. "New White" accents the original plaster frieze.
The armillary sphere points towards the mystery of the galaxies, below. ⁑ The music room glows with color
and is richly layered with furnishings. A willowchair reflects the willow trees outside and
helps downplay the formality of the room. Large stone spheres are echoed by the metal armillary set on
a tall marble pedestal in the center of the room, facing.

White," a perfect complement to the room's cinnabar red accessories; a former servant's room transformed into a storybook castle straight from a fairy tale, filled with pointed finials and children's books and toys and painted in the warm, earthy tones of "String"; and the Venetian bedroom painted in colors of water and light, with "Skylight" blue walls and ceiling and "All White" mantel and trim. A large canopy bed draped with lime green hand-stenciled Scalamandré panels floats like a barge in the center of the room; accents include a crusty Italian chair with its original peeling paint of buttermilk, aqua and Venetian green echoing the room's palette. The layout of the adjoining bathroom, which retained its original fixtures, was kept untouched, but the room was updated with light blue "Skylight" walls and accents of tall, watery green Murano glass vases lined along the mantel.

Every room has a function in the large home and it once again brims with life and laughter, filled with fairy-tale magic thanks to Barry's restoration.

The generous second-floor hall is painted with a calming combination of "Old White" on the walls and ceiling and "Lime White" for the trim. Furniture is a mix of antiques, including a pair of English oak Arts and Crafts consoles, above left. ✥ The cheery citrus palette in the family den ranges from lemon to blood orange, accented by the "Lime White" mantel and woodwork, above right. ✥ Ornate original plaster-work is freshened with "Lime White" and is a pleasing contrast to the original oak woodwork. Eighteenth-century portraits of the de Medici family line the wall, left. ✥ Contrasts of color add excitement to the large rooms and help make their scale more intimate. Harvest oranges and russet reds in the family room add drama to the vista of the dining room beyond, which is painted in appetizing "Cooking Apple Green." Trim is painted "Lime White," facing.

A MURAL OF THE SURROUNDING

countryside is painted on the walls of the master bedroom in sepia tones of
"Dead Salmon," "Smoked Trout," "New White" and "Lime White." The plaster wolfhound is from an old French chateau, facing.
Ellie has her own corner of the chaise in the bedroom, of course. The walls are painted in a mural of sepia-toned Farrow & Ball colors and the
mantel in "New White" with a wash of "Smoked Trout," above left. A glimpse of the bed is seen behind sexy, sheer fabric
panels hung across the round walls of the turret in the master bedroom. The main room is
painted with a mural in Farrow & Ball sepia tones, above right.

"All White" is the perfect counterpoint to the cinnabar red accents in the bedroom. The Victorian papier-mâché dressing table was found in Buenos Aires, left. ❧ The sitting area opposite the beds in the red and white room is a peaceful retreat for guests. Walls, ceiling and trim are simple "All White," and the same color is used in the adjoining bath, which has its original white porcelain fixtures and tile floor, above. ❧ Twin beds in the red and white bedroom, facing, have a quiet Gothic charm, with the walls painted in clean "All White" as to not distract from views of the gardens outside.

Sunlight accents the "All White" mantel and "Skylight" blue walls. A gilded English Regency mirror

reflects light back into the room. The 1920s fabric screen is from a Virginia estate, above. ✥

The Venetian bedroom is painted the colors of water and light: "Skylight" on the walls with

"All White" trim. An Art Deco mirror found in Paris reflects the

crusty buttermilk, aqua and Venetian green paint on an Italian chair found at a country shop—

perfect color complements for the "Skylight" blue walls and ceiling, facing

THE CONNECTING BATH

retains its original tile floor and bath fittings. Walls are painted pale blue "Skylight,"
suggesting a steaming bathtub filled with water. The carved Italian chair with original soft green
paint was found in Sicily, above left. ❧ Generous arched windows frame the view of
the front lawns from the storybook children's room, above right. Filled with finials and spires, it is
straight from a fairy-tale castle. Woodwork is painted in pleasing "String."

THE VENETIAN GLASS

tiles around the connecting bath mantel are original, above left.

❧ A salvaged wooden panel found in Paris was painted in "Skylight," which highlights the

watery greens of Murano and contemporary blown glass vases, above right.

ABE JEROME NEOCLASSICISM IN BROOKLYN

The central rotunda rises three stories and is based on an Adam dining room half-dome at Kedleston Hall in England. Bedrooms on the second and third floors open off the double stairways. Walls are painted warm "Ointment Pink," and the hall and dome ceilings finished in "Parma Gray" for an elegant, neoclassical contrast. Ornamentation and woodwork are painted neutral "Blackened" in an oil eggshell finish for a sophisticated glow, facing. The living room ceiling in "Parma Gray" is reflected in the mirrored coffee table, below.

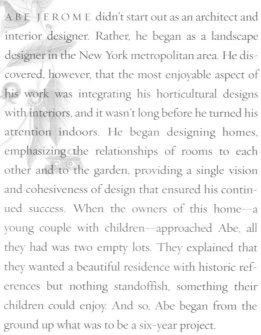

ABE JEROME didn't start out as an architect and interior designer. Rather, he began as a landscape designer in the New York metropolitan area. He discovered, however, that the most enjoyable aspect of his work was integrating his horticultural designs with interiors, and it wasn't long before he turned his attention indoors. He began designing homes, emphasizing the relationships of rooms to each other and to the garden, providing a single vision and cohesiveness of design that ensured his continued success. When the owners of this home—a young couple with children—approached Abe, all they had was two empty lots. They explained that they wanted a beautiful residence with historic references but nothing standoffish, something their children could enjoy. And so, Abe began from the ground up what was to be a six-year project.

The owners wanted the house to be livable, with rooms that were not too large and easily accessible. In response, Abe designed a large entry foyer painted in inviting "Ointment Pink" as the heart of the home, with a double curving staircase and a three-story rotunda. As this took up a large percentage of the home, he then made the remainder of the rooms smaller, on a more human scale. Abe had long been enamored of Robert Adam and neoclassical design,

The intricate detailing of the rotunda dome is taken from Adam's designs and accented with "Blackened." The ceiling is painted in "Parma Gray," a favorite Regency color, and the walls are painted with another classic Regency color, "Ointment Pink."

Adam-inspired ceilings were carried through the main public rooms, and the living room and dining room were designed with plasterwork ceilings based on designs from Adam's London Syon House and painted *Parma Gray* with detailing in *"Blackened".*

so the dome of the rotunda was based on the dining room half-dome at Adam's Kedleston Hall, his eighteenth-century masterpiece in the English countryside; the design for the dome's ornamental frieze was taken from Adam's detailing at Osterley Park. Drawings and clay models of the dome were made, and then the ornate structure itself was constructed from a mixture of plaster, wood composition and resin, which, when painted with Farrow & Ball chalky "Parma Gray" became indistinguishable from plaster. Adam-inspired ceilings were carried through the main public rooms, and the living room and dining room were designed with plasterwork ceilings based on designs from Adam's London Syon House and painted in "Parma Gray" with detailing in "Blackened."

Historic inspiration continued throughout the home: the kitchen ceiling was constructed of handmade tiles designed after a similar ceiling in Vizcaya in southern Florida, and accented with cabinets and walls painted with mellow "Dorset Cream." The Bordeaux Room at the Metropolitan Opera provided inspiration for the master bedroom's reclaimed pine paneling, which was given a light blue wash of "Lulworth Blue" for a feeling of French romanticism. Kykuit, the Rockefeller mansion in the Hudson River Valley in upstate New York, was another favorite source of inspiration. Even the children's rooms were included: one daughter's room was painted in pale "Lulworth Blue," with a striking ceiling patterned after a Sir John Soane design for the Bank of England accented with "Skylight."

The family has lived in the house for more than a year and found it has exceeded their expectations: it envelops its occupants in a warm glow based on the best of romantic classicism yet is still functional, perfect for raising their family.

NEOCLASSICAL SYMMETRY

greets visitors in the entrance foyer with a vista through the house to the rear gardens. Walls are painted in "Ointment Pink," a color used by Adam in the Kedleston Hall library, facing. ✥ Ornate ceiling moldings in the living room are inspired by Robert Adam's Syon House in London. The ceiling is painted "Parma Gray" and the decorative detailing is accented with "Blackened." Gracie wallpaper provides an elegant touch, above.

A half-dome in the master bedroom was inspired by Adam's neoclassical designs and is painted "Ointment Pink," with the molding detailed in "Skylight," above. ✇ The wife's dressing room is also paneled in reclaimed pine that is stained and then washed with "Lulworth Blue," facing top. ✇ An antique wall sconce in the master bedroom is highlighted against the reclaimed pine panels, which were first stained and then lightly washed with "Lulworth Blue" for an elegant Parisian patina, facing bottom.

The dining room's ornate ceiling was inspired by Robert Adam's design for Syon House in London. The ceiling is painted in "Parma Gray" and the molding highlighted with "Blackened." Elegant Gracie wallpaper echoes the crystal and silver accents in the room, left. ❦ The sparkling silver and blue of the wallpaper is reflected in the ornate ceiling, above.

ONE OF THE DAUGHTER'S ROOMS

is painted a pretty "Lulworth Blue" combined with "Skylight" on the ceiling, for a
very light and feminine décor, above. The ceiling design is based on one by Sir John Soane
for the Bank of England. ❧ The master bath is centered on a mosaic
Roman tub with a mosaic half-dome overhead. "Lulworth Blue" polished plaster walls are
hand stenciled in a French neoclassic design, facing.

HANDMADE TILES

Handmade tiles are inset in a reclaimed hickory grid in the kitchen ceiling for an Arts

and Crafts appeal. Their colors are complemented by walls and cabinets painted in "Dorset Cream,"

facing. ❧ The kitchen cabinets are painted "Dorset Cream" and glazed,

creating a warm and welcoming look, above.

Farrow & Ball "All White"
is a clean and neutral backdrop for the
kitchen's collection of colorful
Bauer dishware; the trim is painted with
corresponding "White Tie."
The Aga gives a welcoming note of
English country charm.

KATHRYN M. IRELAND
KITCHEN COLOR IN SANTA MONICA

KATHRYN M. IRELAND is one of southern California's most up-and-coming designers, included in *House and Garden* magazine's "Ten to Watch" list of trendsetters predicted to influence design in the twenty-first century. Kathryn's style is homey and family-friendly, with large doses of color and comfort. Born in England, she came to Los Angeles in 1986, and after opening an accessories shop, Ireland Pays, in 1990 on Santa Monica's Main Street, her interior design business was born. Kathryn launched her own fabric line in 1997 that combines designs from her English background with historic French influences (she has a horse farm in France) and the bohemian lifestyle of the Santa Monica beach.

The kitchen in her own Spanish Revival home in Santa Monica exemplifies her work. Comfortable and unpretentious, it was designed so that everything has a purpose. The house required substantial restoration following the 1994 earthquake, and the kitchen was remodeled in stages as budget allowed. Fitted with dark cabinets and an old linoleum floor, the room was initially brightened with Mexican pavers and painted cabinets; then ten years after work on the house began, the kitchen finally received its own proper remodel. Striving for a clean and uncluttered look, Kathryn removed the upper cabinets, which immediately made the room larger. As she couldn't convince her boys to move to the English countryside, she instead brought it to them with the installation of an English Aga. A colorful Damien Hirst lithograph became the inspiration for the room's color, and to balance its sixty-seven different-colored spots, Kathryn added reproduction Bauer pottery to the open shelves. "Abu," a mellow wine-colored fabric from her fabric line, was used for a simple curtain on the window. Walls were painted with Farrow & Ball "All White" and the trim was finished in "White Tie," for a clean and uncluttered look.

KATHRYN IRELAND'S "ABU" FABRIC,

inspired by Indian designs, adds a dash of color to the window.

"All White" with "White Tie" trim is used throughout the kitchen for a clean, uncluttered background,

above. ❧ The upper kitchen cabinets were removed and open shelving was used to lighten up

the previously dark and crowded walls. "All White" on the walls and "White Tie" for the trim helps

accent the rainbow of color in the tableware, facing.

Painted with "Off-White,"
the original mantelpiece has
delicately carved swirls
that are echoed in the
damask pattern of the
"Silvergate" wallpaper. Some
of Martin's polo trophies
rest on the mantel.

MARTIN EPHSON
UPDATED HAMPSHIRE TRADITION

MARTIN EPHSON, former managing director and co-owner of Farrow & Ball, and his wife, Eugenia, fell in love with Ringwold House on their first visit. The red brick Regency home was sited in a rural Hampshire village near a small village inn, the site of mysterious robberies by a daring highwayman in the late-eighteenth century. On the death of the local squire who lived at Ringwold House, its rooms were discovered to be filled with stolen bounty; thus the mystery of the highwayman was finally solved.

Folklore aside, Martin and Eugenia were attracted by the home's classic proportions. A wide and welcoming central hall opened to large rooms with high ceilings lit by tall, deeply recessed windows with wide window seats. Traditional yet comfortable, the interiors were just lacking a contemporary update. The house was surrounded by three acres of gardens, including an orchard, a thatched summerhouse, colorful herbaceous borders and even paddocks for Martin's polo ponies.

Originally built in the early eighteenth century, with later additions in the nineteenth and twentieth centuries, the house had not been updated, however, since the 1960s and still bore marks of that decade in the form of polystyrene cornices and rooms decorated in avocado and orange. But with the addition of

CALM & TRANQUIL,

the drawing room
is comfortable and inviting papered
with "Silvergate," a nineteenth-century
damask pattern.

The clean look of
"Lime White" walls with
"Off-White"woodwork was
continued to the back
hall as well.

The central hall running the length of the house was painted in *"Lime White,"* the color of bright limewash, and the woodwork was painted in neutral *"Off-White."*

Farrow & Ball paints and wallpapers, the home was soon transformed into a bright and welcoming family retreat.

The central hall running the length of the house was painted in "Lime White," the color of bright limewash, and the woodwork was painted in neutral "Off-White." The drawing room off the main hall was papered in "Silvergate," a two-toned, early-nineteenth-century damask, and accented with "Off-White" for the mantel and woodwork. Calm and tranquil, the room is Martin's favorite spot to relax and yet is perfect for entertaining. The dining room across the hall looks out over the gardens and was painted in "Blue Gray," a complex color that changes hues depending on the light and time of day. A classic eighteenth-century pink and green color scheme was employed—chairs and window seats were upholstered in "Iran," a bright pink floral fabric from Claremont, to contrast with the green of the gardens and walls. The room was anchored by a striking custom rug woven in Katmandu, based, of course, on the Farrow & Ball palette.

In the pantry, which boasts a floor-to-ceiling wine rack, the walls were kept simple with "Off-White" and "Old White" trim. The traditional English kitchen centered on the Aga was also painted in neutral "Off-White," with woodwork accented in "Old White." Upstairs the bedrooms were all wallpapered for intimacy. The master bedroom was hung with "Garland," a dreamy blue and white paper re-created by Farrow & Ball for the restoration of Saltram House in Devon, and woodwork was painted in complementary "Matchstick." The guest room (where a previous occupant wrote the famous TV series *Upstairs, Downstairs*) was papered in springlike "Sweet Pea" and its woodwork and furniture were painted in "Pointing." One of the children's rooms was freshened with the lively sprigs and berries of "Ringwold" paper, inspired by eighteenth-century silk designs.

MARTIN IS AN AVID POLO PLAYER

The "Lime White" walls and "Off-White" woodwork nicely
coordinate with the original stone floors in the hallway, above. ❧ The dining room, facing, is
centered on a custom-woven rug from Katmandu. The influence of outside gardens is brought
indoors with the "Blue Gray" walls accented with "Off-White" woodwork. The table and chairs
were made to Martin's specifications by his cabinetmaker, Nick Coryndon.

THE CENTRAL HALL RUNS

the length of the house. Walls were painted in clear "Lime White" and woodwork was accented in "Off-White" for a bright and welcoming palette, facing. ❧ Detail of the dining room mantel painted in "Off-White" and highlighted by the "Blue Gray" walls that change color with the light and time of day. The serving table was custom made, above.

BISCUIT, THE FAMILY'S TERRIER, HAS A FAVORITE

spot in the kitchen in front of the Aga. Walls are painted with "Off-White" and the woodwork "Old White" for a clean and straightforward appeal, right. ❧ "Off-White" walls in the pantry with "Old White" trim on the shelf anchor the cream and white colors of the food staples, below. ❧ The pantry, facing, holds a floor-to-ceiling wine rack and open shelves of food and supplies. Walls were kept simple in "Off-White" with "Old White" trim.

THE HEADBOARDS

were custom made by Martin's cabinetmaker, facing. ✄

Trailing "Sweet Pea" wallpaper in the guest bedroom is highlighted by woodwork

and furniture painted in "Pointing," above.

"Garland" wallpaper in the master bedroom gives the room a dreamy, romantic appeal. Woodwork was painted in complementary "Matchstick," facing. ❧ A custom headboard, above left, anchors the bed in the master bedroom, which is papered with blue and white "Garland," developed for the restoration of Saltram House in Devon. ❧ The blue and white tassels and swags of the "Garland" wallpaper are reflected in the carving on the gilded, neoclassical sidechair in the master bedroom, above right. ❧ "Ringwold" wallpaper was used to update one of the children's rooms, right.

The entry hall is painted in "Porphyry Pink,"
a popular Regency color often used to highlight architectural
details. A Grand Tour Pompeian vase, seventeenth-century
Khmer pots and votives of amethyst crystal rest on the Anglo-Irish
Regency center table. The brilliant yellow color of the living room
beyond is glimpsed through the archway.

THOMAS M. BEETON
BEL AIR BEAUTY

THOMAS M. BEETON'S background is in both fine antiques and design. Educated at George Washington University, he worked as a designer at Lord & Taylor in New York before moving to southern California as the director of GR Durenberger Antiques in San Juan Capistrano. He opened his own design business based in Los Angeles in 1988. Thomas has won numerous awards for his work, including the Pacific Design Center's Designer of the Year in 2005, and is known for his expert blend of color in traditional design.

When clients in Bel Air began constructing a gracious new home in a parklike setting, Thomas was asked to join architects Tichenor and Thorp to help make it a special space. The public areas—the grand entry hall overlooking the gardens beyond and the adjacent living room—were designed with old-fashioned glamour but with the pop of brilliant, unexpected Farrow & Ball colors: "Porphyry Pink" for the entry hall and brilliant yellow "Babouche" for the living room. Livable and family-oriented, but long on luxury with custom detailing, the welcoming house has a sophistication that makes it look as if had been in the family for generations.

LIGHT AND AIRY YET FULL OF VIBRANT COLOR,

the living room is painted in "Babouche," a deep, confident yellow. An eighteenth-century limestone mantel from France centers the room, while an Italian chandelier of the same period adds a note of elegance overhead. The nineteenth-century Mahal carpet complements and anchors the furnishings.

A Bagues wall sconce in the living room sparkles against the rich yellow walls painted in "Babouche," above left. ❧ Vintage Fortuny fabric shades on an eighteenth-century painted toile wall sconce in the entry perfectly complement the "Porphyry Pink" walls, above right. ❧ A corner of the living room draws interest with a nineteenth-century French oil and a handsome commode by Stefan Boudin for Maison Jansen, c. 1950, left. "Babouche" was chosen for the walls for its deep, sunlight color during the day and its even deeper candlelight quality at night. ❧ Detail of an English Regency bench in the entry hall and an eighteenth-century gilded mirror, highlighted against the rosy "Porphyry Pink" walls, facing.

A gracious
entry hall sets the tone
for the apartment, whose
paneling and trim
are painted in Farrow & Ball
"Off-White."

SUSAN BEIMLER
CLASSIC ELEGANCE ON LAKE SHORE DRIVE

SUSAN BEIMLER shares her design business with her daughter Alison, and, while based in Washington, D.C., has clients across the country. Her simple and straightforward design philosophy is undoubtedly what makes her so successful: she strives for authenticity, warmth and comfort and makes sure to communicate clearly. The apartment in Chicago is, in fact, the third home she has done for this client—a testament to Susan's design skill and acumen.

Fifteen hundred Lake Shore Drive is considered one of Chicago's most desirable addresses and has had many illustrious residents, such as William Wrigley, Jr., since it was completed in 1929. McNally & Quinn and Rosario Candela from New York designed the twenty-five-story building in the French Renaissance style. Large and spacious apartments have sweeping views of Lake Michigan, which is what attracted Susan's client to the building when she decided to simplify her life and move back to downtown Chicago.

Previous owners had not significantly altered the apartment and, luckily, its good bones remained intact; aside from the addition of more substantial moldings, no new construction was required. The layout and traffic flow were well thought out. A gracious entry hall with a striking vaulted ceiling set the tone of the apartment, and its wainscot paneling and moldings were painted with Farrow & Ball "Off-White." The walls of the large living room were painted with "Matchstick,"

a warm beige—as a pleasing background to complement the antiques and comfortable furnishings while allowing the eye to be drawn to the blue serenity of Lake Michigan views outside. Accents such as pillows made from antique Aubusson and Fortuny fabrics added subtle notes of color and pattern. The adjoining dining room was designed to be as comfortable, its Directoire dining table flanked by a pair of generous wing chairs. Walls were painted with a warm brown "Dauphin" to accent the beautiful tones of the dining table and buffet. Additional rooms in the ten-room apartment include a sunny and sweet guest room, which was painted in Farrow & Ball warm "Cream," the perfect complement to the cheerful draperies and textiles used throughout the room.

THE LARGE LIVING ROOM

features a wide bank of windows with a spectacular view. Walls are painted with "Matchstick," a pleasing complement

to both the furnishings and the serenity of the blue waters of Lake Michigan. Tailored window treatments in a light celadon silk from Rogers

and Goffigon frame the view, above. ❧ The pale beige "Matchstick" color on the walls highlights antique furnishings

in the living room, including antique crystal decanters and a gilded mirror, facing inset.

THE DINING ROOM

is painted in "Dauphin" for a warm
and sophisticated look. The rich wood tones of the
antique Directoire dining table and buffet are
accented nicely by the color of the walls.

W arm "Cream" walls accent the bright colors of antique French porcelain in the guest bedroom. The sunny guest room is painted with "Cream," which harmonizes well with the cheerful fabrics used throughout the room.

Farrow & Ball "Pointing" was used
for the eighteenth-century-style paneling, trim and ceiling in the new
entrance hall and on the staircase leading to the guest wing.
"Plain Stripes ST1142" wallpaper in two tones of soft, jolly yellow wakes up the
somewhat dim area during the day and turns it into a glowing,
golden space at night. Snowshoes are used by winter guests.

JULIA WEST
COMFORT CANADIAN STYLE

JULIA WEST loves to solve problems. After earning her law degree, she practiced as a barrister in Toronto for twenty years until she decided to follow her muse and open her own design business in 1998. Julia has an extraordinary eye for color and texture and has developed her own highly successful line of beautifully embroidered bed linens, crisply tailored pillows and other soft furnishing accessories, along with custom-designed furniture. Julia finds the analytical skills that she developed while practicing law are just what she needs to solve often-complex and intricate design dilemmas, whether it's developing a Gustavian-inspired cabinet to camouflage a computer or selecting just the right colors for an interior. She was able to show her design skill and acumen to its fullest when asked to renovate a country home in the softly rolling Caledon Hills outside of Toronto.

Built in the 1850s, the simple fieldstone farmhouse had a classic English Regency elegance in its structure and interiors that Julia wanted to preserve. Used as a weekend and summer home, it needed to be comfortable and able to accommodate guests. Working with architect Anthony Belcher, Julia designed a new kitchen, dining

LIGHT GRAY

"Hardwick White"
gives the guest bath the cool look of
stone to complement the white
"Pointing" on the trim and ceiling.
Pillows in gentlemanly
flannel and tweed fabrics usually
reserved for men's coats
(from Julia West Home) give the
room an air of masculine
sophistication.

An alcove under the eaves is transformed into a reading nook or just a quiet spot for daydreaming, with built-in steps and cabinets painted in "Pointing." Walls are restful "Parma Gray," its blue tones accented with blue and white boxes, books and pillows.

Millwork was done in a combination of colonial and historic revival styles based on inspirations as diverse as *Thomas Jefferson's Monticello* and an Arts and Crafts Scottish inn.

room/library, bathroom and guest room but took care to not overshadow the original footprint of the house, perfectly sited almost as a sculptural element in the landscape. Thus, additions were planned to follow the layout of the land, enabling the addition of another story without altering the original rooflines.

Interior details were kept simple and made to look as if the home had evolved over time. Millwork was done in a combination of colonial and historic revival styles based on inspirations as diverse as Thomas Jefferson's Monticello and a Scottish Arts and Crafts inn. Colors were kept soft and rural—"Pointing," "Hardwick White," "New White," "Farrow's Cream" and "Parma Gray"— but accented with a few surprises: a periwinkle blue "Viola" island in the kitchen, dark brown "Mahogany" in the pantry to showcase the beautiful woodwork and stemware, and a cheerful red stripe-on-stripe wallpaper ("Plain Stripe 1134") in the mudroom to help

warm chilly fingers and toes after a frosty afternoon of snowshoeing. A cache of antique embroidered French linen was gathered and used liberally for curtains, bedcovers, loose chair slipcovers and tablecloths, adding a subtle sense of comfort and wear. Furniture was designed by Julia and made in her workshops: a kitchen pantry from old convent doors, comfortable beds and armchairs to sink into for a good read or a snooze. The overall effect is warm and inviting, exuding a classical sense of timeless comfort, Canadian style.

DETAILING ON THE MANTEL

in the sitting room is crisp and fresh in "Pointing," facing.

❦ An old crackled chest of drawers highlights the design of "St Antoine" damask wallpaper in the

guest bedroom. The intimate paper, whose design was taken from a 1793

French damask, gives the room the appeal of a vernacular English country cottage, above.

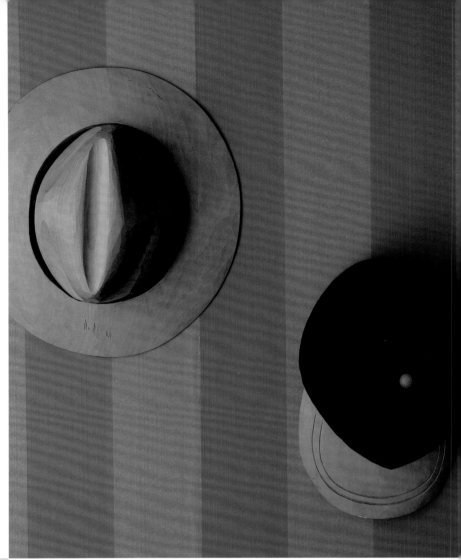

"Plain Stripes ST1142" in buttery yellows in the entrance hall is contrasted against the same "Plain Stripes ST1134" paper in warm reds in the mudroom. The pantry is seen beyond. "Pointing" is used for the woodwork, left. ❧ For a whimsical touch in the mudroom, wooden hats hand carved by a Montreal artist hang on the wall, above. ❧ "Plain Stripes ST1142" wallpaper is used in the upper hall of the new addition in a cheerful yellow shade, for a fresh and welcoming look. Here the guest bedroom under the eaves beckons through the romantically arched doorway. "Pointing" is used for the woodwork and ceiling throughout, facing.

ulia wanted to bring the surrounding gardens
and porches inside the dining room, so she
painted the walls "Cooking Apple Green," and
the ceiling in light blue "Parma Gray." She
continued the "Parma Gray" out onto the
bead board ceilings of two adjacent porches.
The sitting room is seen through a progres-
sion of rooms and levels in the old farmhouse,
left. ✖ The dining room shows the old-fashioned "Cooking Apple Green" walls echoed in
the flowers, above.

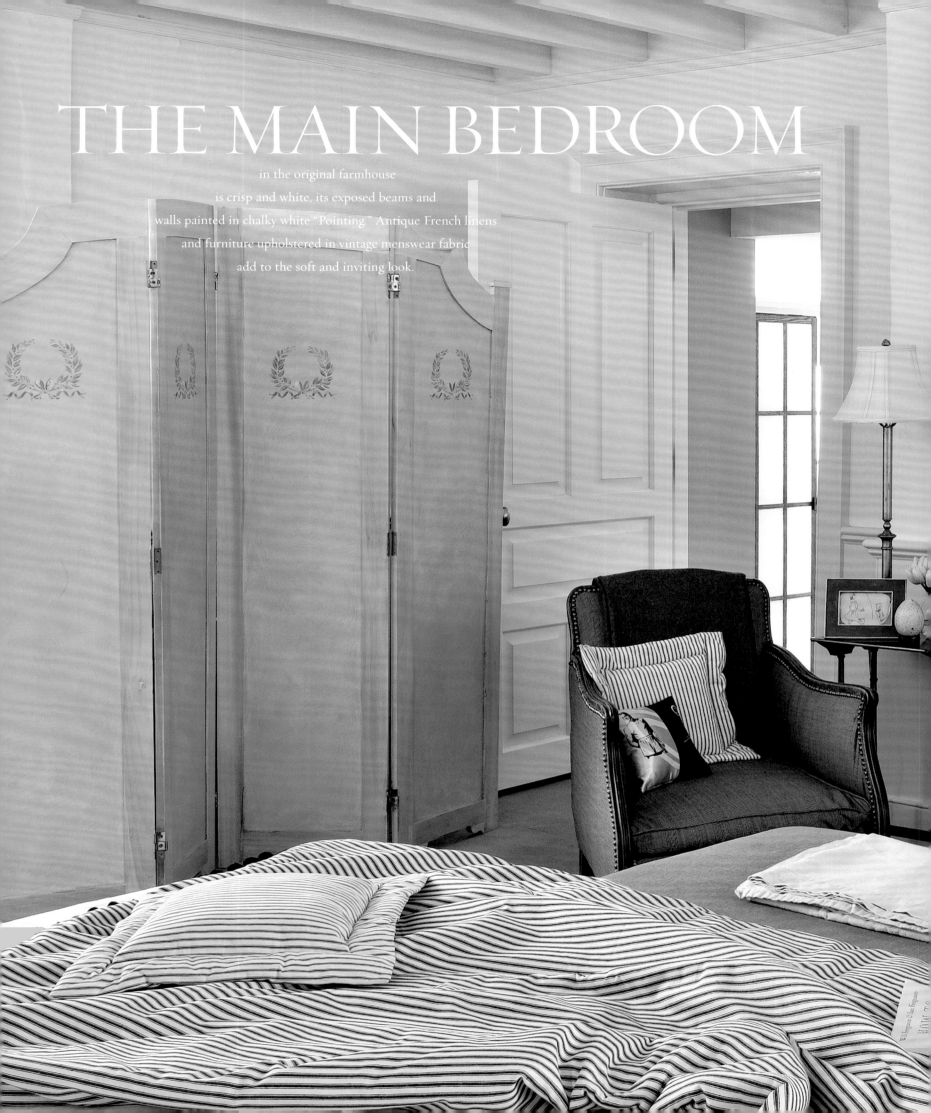

THE MAIN BEDROOM

in the original farmhouse
is crisp and white, its exposed beams and
walls painted in chalky white "Pointing." Antique French linens
and furniture upholstered in vintage menswear fabric
add to the soft and inviting look.

BLACK AND WHITE SILHOUETTES

highlighted against the simple white "Pointing" on the mantel

keep the room sharp and focused, above. ❧ Starched white French linens

stacked on a chair in the master bedroom echo the white "Pointing"

of the walls and woodwork, facing.

The walls of the small but open pantry are painted with dramatic "Mahogany," whose rich chocolate brown is an effective background for highlighting the dinnerware. Flower arrangements are done at the sink, where the cabinetry is simply painted "New White" and "Pointing," facing. ✵ Stemware sparkles against the deep brown "Mahogany" used on the walls of the open pantry shelves, above. ✵ A corner cabinet in the kitchen is stried with "Cook's Blue." The walls are painted in "Farrow's Cream," which nicely complements the wonderful, musty backgrounds of the nineteenth-century silhouettes hanging on the wall, right.

The heart of the home is the large new country kitchen with walls painted in "Farrow's Cream," cabinetry in "New White" and trim in "Pointing." The room's design was inspired by an eighteenth-century kitchen Julia visited at a National Trust house in Cornwall with large, high windows and long center tables. Julia decided to abandon her usual reserve and painted the center island a striking periwinkle "Viola" for a splash of fresh, country color. Note the large-scale herringbone-patterned floor that was custom made, based on a venerable floor seen at

a textiles museum in France. The table at the window was made by Mennonite carpenters to Julia's design, above. ❧ The kitchen is painted in tones of clotted cream: "Farrow's Cream" on the walls, "New White" on the cabinetry and "Pointing" for the trim, above right. ❧ Detail of the kitchen mantel over the stove painted in clean, crisp "New White," below right.

EMMA JANE PILKINGTON
LIGHT AND SCALE IN MANHATTAN

EMMA JANE PILKINGTON, born in Melbourne, Australia, and raised there and in Greenwich, Connecticut, has been designing fine interiors in the New York City area since 1995. Named one of the top "50 Tastemakers" by *House and Garden* magazine in 2005, her work has been featured in many national and international publications. Emma admits that her design approach is primarily guided by instinct as she looks for the intrinsic balance and harmony of each space; she likes to balance the lyrical with the classic and never lets a space appear too studied. Passionate about fine antiques, Emma designs like a collector yet strives to incorporate classic treasures in modern and unexpected ways.

Emma is known for her creative use of color. It is thus a bit of a surprise to visit her own prewar apartment on New York's fashionable Sutton Place, bordering the East River, and see it painted completely in varying tones of gray and white with just three main Farrow & Ball colors: "Pointing," "Lamp Room Gray" and "Blackened." (Accents of "Off-Black Oil" were also added as highlights throughout the apartment.) The simple yet subtle palette creates the perfect backdrop for Emma's collection of striking artwork and antiques, as well as making the rooms a cozy cocoon for her family. Hand-painted floors based on classic

Detail of a circa 1780 Swedish painted mirror in the
bathroom. The original paint on this mirror in matte white and black is the perfect complement for
walls lacquered in high gloss "Blackened," below. ✄ The powder room is reflected in its mirrored door and sparkles with
white, high-gloss "Blackened" on the walls. "Blackened" reinforces the matte white of the plaster
neoclassical ceiling fixture, adding to the dramatic effect. Honed Carrera and nero marquina marble walls and
a classic mosaic marble floor add subtle notes of color, facing.

marquetry designs, using geometric and stylized acanthus motifs, add pleasing notes of design and contrast to the otherwise quiet and studied interiors.

While Emma and her husband were first attracted to the good bones of the apartment with its large, light-filled rooms and classic Candela design, it nonetheless required a substantial, two-year renovation. Original details were carefully preserved, from molding and trim to door hardware, while at the same time updated systems were installed to protect the art and fine antiques and bring the apartment into the twenty-first century.

Farrow & Ball matte white "Pointing" was selected for the walls, plaster crown moldings and baseboards in most of the rooms. In the dining room, "Pointing" in high gloss was chosen to create a sexier look, helping to set the stage for those sophisticated dinner parties for which New York is so famous. The dining room was transformed into an essay of light, with an eight-foot, sparkling and twisting silver Verner Panton sculpture hung across one wall and a pair of large crystal chandeliers glistening overhead; a massive mirror at the opposite end of the room bounces the reflections of the sculpture and chandeliers back into the room. Colors are varied by the simple addition of flowers, china and linens.

The master bedroom, meanwhile, was painted in peaceful Farrow & Ball "Blackened," the perfect backdrop for

the room's painted furniture. Emma varies the room's palette with her choice of bed linens. Both bathrooms are also painted with "Blackened" in high gloss, the color changing subtly with reflections of the different hues in the marble walls and cabinetry (painted in oil eggshell "Pointing") and thus harmonizing beautifully with both. Emma used her collection of fine antique mirrors to both inspire and complement her choices within the limited color palette of each room. The apartment now sparkles with light and the subtle yet ever-changing tones of white and gray.

The silk interior of the burled walnut secretary in the living room is painted with matte "Off-Black Oil" to absorb all light, thus emphasizing the light bouncing off the collection of crystal, Buccellati silver and Nymphenburg porcelain. "Off-Black Oil" was used as an accent color throughout the apartment to complement the antique ebonized pieces, left. ❧ The living room light is diffused with "Pointing" on the walls, turning it into a study in light and dark. The bronze sculpture *L'Ebryon*, by Mauro Corda, rests on a large, ebonized, circa 1810 Anglo-Indian center table from a Rajastani palace, facing.

Detail of a circa 1840 Venetian glass mirror in the living room, which creates colors where there were none by reflecting the matte walls through its various smoky and etched surfaces.

"Blackened" in a matte finish was chosen for the bedroom walls for its restfulness and its reaction with the light—it changes from a dusty green-gray to a very pale shade of purple. The bed and companion armoire were stripped and lacquered in "Pigeon," inspired by the original finish on the circa 1810 painted-wood English chandelier, and then waxed to achieve a classic French painted effect., left. ❧ Detail of bedpost painted in "Pigeon," above.

THE LIGHT BOUNCES OFF THE HIGHLY

polished spheres of the C. Jere sculpture in the living room, highlighting "Pointing" walls in matte
Estate® Emulsion, above left. ❧ The "Lamp Room Gray" walls in the study, above right, are applied in matte Estate® Emulsion to create a
serene and restful room. The cabinetry is painted in oil-based "Pointing" with "Off-Black" detail. This combination is echoed and
inspired by the eighteenth-century Directoire daybed. The important Dominique desk and chairs are a high-sheen black that plays
against the c. 1815 Directoire chandelier with its original painted finish. ❧ A massive painted Georgian mirror in the study
reflects the "Lamp Room Gray" walls in its mottled surface. The chandelier echoes the
colors of the room with its original painted surface, facing.

In the dining room, facing, the light from a pair of chandeliers is captured in a huge eighteenth-century Italian mirror. The black Chinese cabinets are in stark contrast to the walls, lacquered in eight coats of "Pointing." A collection of eighteenth-century candlesticks includes candles from the family's candle company. ❦ The silvered spirals of the Verner Panton sculpture reflect light and create even more movement against the lacquered walls, above left. ❦ A collection of mushroom prints, c. 1815, gives color and movement in the butler's pantry, above right. All the cabinetry is painted with "All-White Oil Eggshell." ❦ The living room walls are painted in "Pointing" as a neutral backdrop for the fine antiques, including a Regency zograscope (developed to magnify the details in etchings in the early nineteenth century). A collection of vintage Buccellati silver sits atop a Tric Trac table, c. 1760, that serves as a coffee table when not in use, right.

A barrel-vaulted ceiling
adds a dramatic accent to the central hall.
Columns and walls are painted
with "Farrow's Cream" for a simple yet
warm and inviting palette. The family
room is seen beyond.

Cathy Kincaid
Mediterranean
Simplicity in Dallas

DISCUSS DALLAS and interior design and the name Cathy Kincaid is soon mentioned. A native Texan, she has had her own design firm there since 1978 and is known for her comfortable, calm and sophisticated style. Cathy's forte is her eye for color—her expert weaving of tones throughout an interior, giving rooms a common thread with unexpected and exciting accents. Cathy works closely with her associate Betsy Massey creating many of Dallas's most beautiful homes.

When the owners of this gracious Mediterranean villa in Dallas contacted Cathy, they explained that their newly purchased house was ideal for their needs; with its large, open rooms and loggia overlooking the backyard pool, it was well suited to entertaining and hosting charity events. The heavily carved interiors, decorated with pickled woodwork, however, did not match their furnishings or décor. Cathy's approach was simple and straightforward: unify the house with paint and color rather than attempt to reconstruct it.

Centered on the grand, vaulted foyer, the rooms were made more cohesive with a clear, bright palette of Farrow & Ball "Farrow's Cream" on the walls and "Pale Powder" on the ceilings. The soft blue "Pale Powder" was continued in the dining room, where it was applied to the ceiling in a gloss that reflects light back into the room. In the main salon, walls were painted a complementary "Off-White" to accent the owners' collection of blue and white export china. And in the large kitchen, a pleasing combination of "French Gray" for the cabinets and "String" for the walls was chosen for an inviting, more cohesive look. Woodwork in the upstairs master bedroom was accented with "Pointing," which was continued onto the cabinets of the adjoining master bath for a more consistent reinterpretation of the rooms. Calm, cool and unified, the house now reflects its owners perfectly.

ARCHED, GLASS POCKET DOORS

painted in "Farrow's Cream" open off the main hall into the dining room.
Walls in the dining room are given a dull glaze of "Pale Powder," while the ceiling is highlighted
with "Pale Powder" in gloss. Accents of antique creamware plates on the
walls carry the cream palette into the room from the hallway outside, facing. ✥ The main staircase
sweeps upstairs and is lit by a skylight, above. Walls and molding details are simplified with
"Farrow's Cream." The ceiling is accented with soft blue "Pale Powder."

THE MAIN SALON IS PAINTED IN

glossy "Off-White" and the ceiling in "Pale Powder" to accent the owners' collection of antique blue and white export china. Custom furniture is comfortably mixed with family pieces such as a Regency armchair; a French linen carpet by Stark anchors the room. Window treatments are kept simple to minimize the architecture and emphasize the room's soft appeal.

"Farrow's Cream" woodwork coordinates a built-in bar underneath the vaulted ceiling with the rest of the hall. A collection of twelve botanical engravings draws the eye back into the space, above. ⚜ The family room at the back of the central hall leads onto the loggia. The walls are continued in "Farrow's Cream," while the ceiling is darkened slightly with "Blue Gray," facing.

The loggia is used for entertaining year-round. The carved wooden mantel is painted with cool "Wall White," as are the arched French glass doors, facing. ✺ Detail of the loggia's carved wooden mantel highlighted with simple "Wall White," right.

RATHER THAN COMPLETELY

remodeling the kitchen, it was revitalized with unifying "French Gray" on the

cabinets and "String" on the walls and ceiling, facing. ❧ Detail of the kitchen mantel painted with

"French Gray" and complemented by neutral "String" on the walls, above.

The master bath was not remodeled but rather coordinated with color by painting the cabinets, walls and woodwork with "Pointing," left. ❧ The master bedroom woodwork is painted with "Pointing" as well. Gracie wallpaper covers the walls, above.

The dining room
is painted with a striking,
whimsically naïve mural. The
ceiling is painted with
"Pointing" in gloss to reflect
light into the room;
woodwork is painted with
"All White."

CATHY KINCAID
PRESERVATION DALLAS STYLE

WHILE DALLAS is known for its grand residences, some of the most charming and historic homes were more intimate residences designed in the 1920s by famed architect Hal Thompson. This Thompson home built in 1921 features many of his signature details, including beautiful hardwood floors, ornate moldings and a classic symmetry of design. Even the original clapboards on the graceful American Colonial exterior were still intact and were, in fact, what sold the house to the current owner, as they reminded him of his Virginia childhood.

Retaining the layout of the house, Cathy used color and comfort to bring the house forward into the current owners' lifestyle. The small entry with a fireplace (unusual for Dallas) set the tone and was updated with walls painted in cheerful "Dayroom Yellow" and woodwork accented with versatile, stone-colored "Clunch." The living room was kept cozy with glazed walls of old-fashioned, distemper-inspired "Ball Green" overglazed with "Green Stone" for depth and character. Woodwork—including wonderful, oversized folding interior window shutters—was accented with soft, off-white "Clunch." The dining room on the opposite side of the entry hall was enlivened with a striking, naïve Raj-style mural, while the woodwork was dressed simply in "All White."

A powder room on the main floor was customized with faux bois walls painted in knotty pine, with a basecoat of "Cream" and an overglaze of "Straw" in satin finish. The same treatment was continued in the master bedroom upstairs, whose walls were paneled and then painted with knotty pine in a faux bois "Cream" and "Straw" application to create the charm of an English country house.

The kitchen was the only room in the home that was remodeled. Gutted and redesigned by architect Wilson Fuqua, it was inspired by Swedish interiors; pale tea and cream palette of antique Delft tiles applied over the stove. Walls were painted in soft blue "Pale Powder" and cabinets in complementary "Off-White."

The intimate entry hall is painted in clear, bright "Dayroom Yellow," with woodwork in "Clunch" to make the space
welcoming and cheerful. It is now one of the owner's favorite spots to relax and open the morning mail, above. ❧ The garden colors surrounding the house
are brought indoors with soft green walls of "Ball Green" overglazed with "Green Stone" and "Clunch" on the woodwork.
Custom lamp shades were designed by Charles Birdsong, facing.

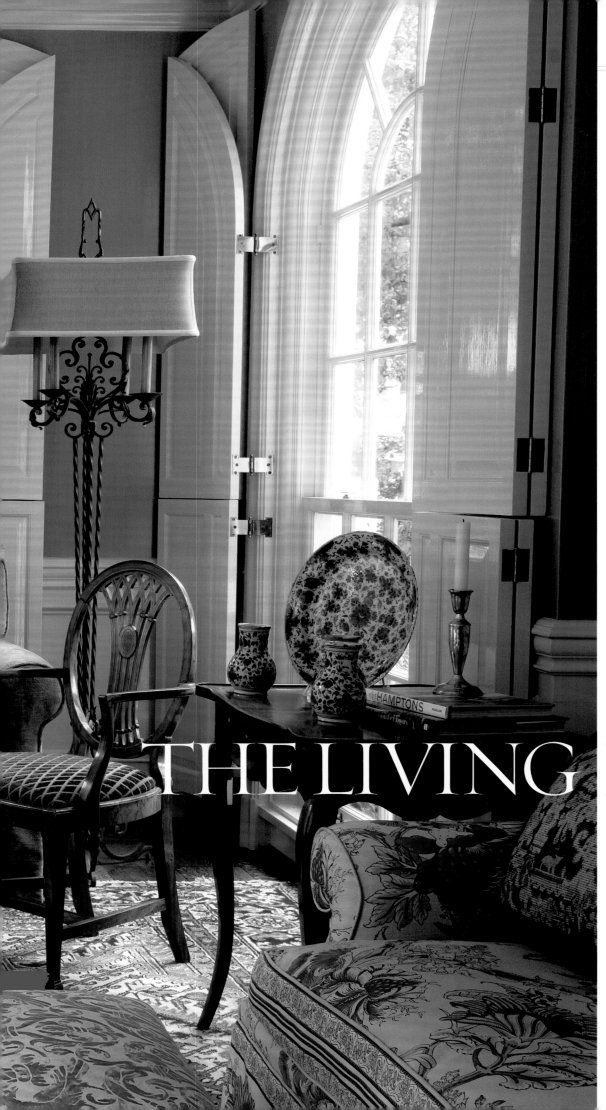

THE LIVING ROOM

is made intimate with walls
painted in distemper-inspired "Ball Green"
with an overglaze of "Green Stone."
The striking woodwork, including folding
inside shutters, is accented
with neutral "Clunch."

The master bedroom has the look of an English country house with paneling painted a faux bois knotty pine in "Cream" and "Straw." Chelsea Editions fabric adds to the English ambience, above. ⚓ The powder room has the look of a yacht, left. ⚓ The bedroom mantel is a detailed look at the faux bois painting, all in "Cream" and "Straw," facing.

THE KITCHEN, OVERLOOKING THE BACKYARD

and pool, was completely remodeled. A palette of light cream and blue is used, with "Pale Powder" on the walls and "Off-White" on the cabinets; the ceiling is treated with a mixture of both in gloss. A pair of antique tole chandeliers hangs overhead, left. ❧ A breakfast nook in the kitchen, with the bead board woodwork painted "Pale Powder" blue, below.

Bowls and cartons of eggs are
stored in the pantry. The far room is
papered in " Snail" and the front room in
"Jasmine" for a sweet country appeal.
The woodwork is "Off-White," facing. ❧
Horses and stables
are very much a part of the home, below.

TOM HELME
ENGLISH COUNTRYSIDE CHARM

TOM HELME, former joint owner and managing director of Farrow & Ball, has always had a passion for the past. Before Farrow & Ball, he was an interior designer specializing in historic houses and worked with the National Trust developing their line of historic paints. His own home in the picturesque countryside of southwest England shows his unsurpassed eye for color and design at its best. Mount Orleans was one of three working farms built for Lord Elsbury as a tribute to his three sons who fought in the Battle of Waterloo. Patterned after farms in France, Mount Orleans was constructed as a quadrangle of buildings around a central courtyard. A four-bedroom stone farmhouse has remained the main family residence, updated with additions of another wing and recently an indoor swimming pool. Across the courtyard to the southwest, Tom converted a feed barn into his studio, removing the bins and painting the planking and floors simple "Off-White."

The main house, decorated entirely with Farrow & Ball paints and papers, seems as if it has been in the family for generations. The two-story boot room off the main door, originally the laundry room, "has been kept clean and basic," painted in "Old White" and the woodwork is "Off-White." An adjacent two-room pantry used to store eggs from the farm's many hens

is papered in "Jasmine" and "Snail," for a simple country appeal. The breakfast room is also papered, in cool blue ground and white "Block Print Stripe," and the floor and woodwork received "Off-White" for a Gustavian elegance. The drawing room is painted in "Blue Gray," a pleasing backdrop for Tom's eclectic collection of art, books and objects collected on travels around the world. The dining room (originally the kitchen) is cozy and inviting in "Entrance Hall Pink," which accents the scenic blue and white tiles surrounding the Aga.

Tom had previously worked closely with the National Trust to restore several attic rooms at Kingston Lacy, which had originally been designed to look like campaign tents to honor the visiting Duke of Wellington after the Battle of Waterloo. Tom replicated the same striped papers and red rope trim in his own master bath and dressing room with the cream and deep blue stripes of "Tented Stripe." The most recent addition to the home is a grand indoor swimming pool contained in a glass-walled pool house set amongst the gardens behind the main house block. Anchored by a roof that simulates the curved hull of a ship and painted in "Pointing," the pool house gives off an ethereal glow with "Borrowed Light" to reflect the pale blue waters of the pool.

THE DRAWING ROOM

is a pleasing "Blue Gray" with "Off-White" woodwork to complement Tom's collection of books and
objets d'arts, above left. ❧ Calm and restful "Blue Gray" is continued in the back hall and the staircase, above right. ❧ "Blue Gray" is a
complementary backdrop for a collection of antiques and art in the drawing room, below right.

T
he boot room off the main entry is a vital
part of the home, which it is still a working farm
with horses, chickens and exotic roosters.
Originally the laundry room, the walls here are
clean with "Old White" paint accented with
"Off-White" woodwork, facing. ❧ A curious
rooster peers into the pantry, where eggs are
lined up in cartons on the counter, their tan and
creamy whites coordinating nicely with the
"Jasmine" wallpaper. Woodwork is, again, "Off-
White," above left. ❧ Eggs in creamy whites,
tans and blues echo the pantry's color palette,
above right. ❧ A pheasant in the backyard is
framed thru the pantry window, whose trim is
painted in "Off-White," below right.

A CABIN BEDROOM

with a built-in bed and shelves is painted in neutral

"Off-White," facing. ✖ A cabin bathroom is clean and straightforward with "Off-White"

walls and woodwork. The adjoining red and white guest bedroom

is papered in "Brockhampton Star," following suit of Tom and his wife Mirabel's first bedroom in

London. Bed linens are eighteenth-century toiles found at Portobello, above.

The dining room mantel painted in "Off-White" is contrasted against warm "Entrance Hall Pink" walls, above. The dining room in the middle of the house was originally the home's kitchen and is centered on a large mantel and Aga. Walls are painted "Entrance Hall Pink" for a softer, more intimate feel, right.

om's bathroom and adjoining dressing room, facing, are papered in blue and white "Tented Stripe," which he developed while restoring a historic room designed with this pattern for a visit by the Duke of Wellington after Waterloo. ❧ Tom created his studio in the feed barn and painted the walls and woodwork straightforward "Off-White," above. ❧ A screen of eighteenth-century Dufour wallpaper was the basis for the "Four Seasons" paper that hangs on the walls of the master bedroom, right.

"BLOCK PRINT STRIPE"

in blue and white in the breakfast room gives it a Gustavian sensibility.

The painting, c. 1940, is by a relative of Tom's, above. ❧ The breakfast room is papered in

white and blue "Block Print Stripe," while the woodwork and floor are painted

"Off-White" for a clean and crisp appeal, facing.

The pool house is set amongst the gardens. Its ceiling is shaped like the hull of a ship and painted in "Pointing." Walls are painted light blue "Borrowed Light," above. ❧ A changing room in the pool house is painted with powder blue walls of "Borrowed Light" and the woodwork in "Pointing," echoing the pool waters, facing above. ❧ An abstract painting in Farrow & Ball colors highlights a "Pointing"-painted bench in the pool house, facing below.

The breakfast room
is where the family gathers,
so "Green Stone"
was chosen for its tranquil
tones. "Strong White" on the
trim is echoed in the
draperies, which frame views
of the swimming pool and
valleys beyond.

SARAH CHAVEZ
L.A. HIP

SARAH CHAVEZ is not your traditional designer—she does not do chintz. Raised in L.A., she cites Hollywood studio glamour, the Counterculture movement of the seventies and eighties, punk rock and skateboarding as her influences. Sarah has worked in fashion photography and interior design for nearly three decades and studied interior design at UCLA. With her design partner Marina Mizruh, she runs her successful design business, Chimera Interiors, in Los Angeles. While her work tends to be hip and cutting edge, Sarah's philosophy is that mainstream: decoration is meant to inspire and enhance but should never be superfluous—don't be afraid to exercise restraint.

When clients asked Sarah to help make their Beverly Park home in the hills above Los Angeles more cohesive, they specified a stylish but low-key approach. The breakfast room is where the busy family spends most of its time at home, so Sarah began with the room's color, selecting Farrow & Ball "Green Stone" for its tranquility—a prized commodity in the sometimes chaotic household. After that, everything fell into place—draperies in off-white and acid green natural linen were created to echo the "Strong White" color chosen for the woodwork and to frame the views of the swimming pool and valley beyond. Furniture pieces, including movable ottoman cubes upholstered in cream-colored leather, were versatile choices for the active family. The wife collects Asian art, so Sarah lined a collection of stone Buddha heads along one counter, making a statement of serenity and peace.

The oldest son, a bright and sophisticated twelve-year-old, was very involved in the design of his room. He wanted a hip yet comfortable space—a place to study, practice music and entertain his friends. He chose a striped wall-to-wall carpet from Westwood whose warm, organic tones inspired the use of "Hay," a bright but not overly strong Farrow & Ball yellow, for the walls. Chocolate brown-and-white retro accent pillows, along with a pair of stylized vinyl olive trees appliquéd on the wall above the headboard, gave the room just the right amount of flair.

Inspired by design great David Hicks, Sarah created a dining room that is at once glamorous

and playful, yet intimate. Walls are lacquered with "Mahogany" and woodwork is trimmed with "All White." More Buddhas pronounce a note of tranquility. Vintage furnishings from the sixties and seventies were found—a crystal chandelier, a pair of neoclassical lamps and crystal candlesticks. A mirror salvaged from the Beverly Hills Hotel hangs on the wall, reflecting light back into the room.

The twelve-year-old son's room is painted in a warm palette of yellow "Hay" to coordinate with the earth tones of the striped carpet. A vinyl appliqué of stylized olive trees found in Paris and retro pillows from Jonathan Adler in chocolate and white are hip and amusing accents.

The dining room has a theme of Hollywood glamour, with rich, lacquered "Mahogany" walls accented in "All White" woodwork making the claim. Furnishings include a custom crystal chandelier inspired by the sixties and dining room chairs upholstered in metallic pewter leather, above.
❧ "Mahogany" lacquered walls and "All White" woodwork set a perfect stage for a collection of Buddhas. Vintage neoclassical lamps from the seventies are an elegant accent on the lacquered buffet, facing above. ❧ A mirror salvaged from the Beverly Hills Hotel reflects the sparkling crystal chandelier back into the room. The ebonized Mente Verdi Young dining table is from the seventies, facing below.

John Lyle and Mark Umbach A Seaside Guest Cottage in Maine

The dining room mantel and paneled wall behind are painted in brilliant "Rectory Red." The bull's-eye gilded mirror is American, c. 1850. French doors open to a wide verandah overlooking the ocean.

JOHN LYLE and Mark Umbach have been partners in their successful design firm, Lyle and Umbach, Ltd., since 1985. Trained as an artist, John's sculptures and interior design work have been featured in many publications, and together, he and Mark produce a line of home furnishings ranging from hand-cast andirons to custom lighting that is carried in showrooms around the country. Mark spends most of his time in a rambling shingled cottage on an island off the coast of Maine, and the two are frequently asked to collaborate on projects in the area. Attention to hand craftsmanship and detail combined with an unerring sense of color and proportion are their hallmarks, qualities shown at their best in two recent restorations for island neighbors.

The first project, a large, early-twentieth-century stable and garage, had been already remodeled by its owners—rotated on its site so it overlooked the ocean and extensively enlarged into comfortable guest quarters. Details, including the sturdy original ceiling beams and posts, were carefully preserved to honor the home's origins. John helped bring a sense of warmth and intimacy to the rooms with the addition of Farrow & Ball color and wallpaper. In the dining room, the intimate patterns of "St Antoine" damask wallpaper and the glow of

"Rectory Red" paint on the mantel give the room a warmth and charm that are perfect for long, candlelight dinners in front of the fire while listening to the waves crash on the beach below.

In the kitchen, which overlooks the sea, cheerful Farrow & Ball "Tented Stripe" in a sunny yellow and red starts the day off right. Thirty-foot-tall ceilings from the original stables crown the upstairs family room, and Farrow & Ball "Citron" and "Dayroom Yellow" were mixed together to create a cozy yellow glow and help give the room a more human scale.

John and Mark designed much of the furniture as well, from the comfortably upholstered dining room armchairs accented with custom fringe to the sleekly stylish sofas and chairs slipcovered in crisp white linen in the family room.

Whether it's a brilliant summer day spent watching the ocean waves or a foggy autumn afternoon playing chess around the fireplace, the house is a warm and inviting retreat for those lucky guests who come to Maine for a visit.

THE DINING ROOM

is the center of the house.
Walls are papered with Farrow & Ball
"St Antoine" damask, which coordinates
well with the fiery "Rectory Red"
mantel. Upholstered chairs and
the striking overhead chandelier were
custom made in the Lyle and
Umbach workshop.

A ROUND, CUSTOM-BRAIDED WOOL RUG

anchors the kitchen, which is papered in sunny yellow and red "Tented Stripe."

The dining room beyond glows with a "Rectory Red" mantel. The living room can be glimpsed in the background,

its walls painted with a combination of "Citron" and "Dayroom," above. ❧ The upper story of the

cottage retains its original posts and beams. Soaring ceilings are balanced by walls painted in "Dayroom Yellow" and

"Citron," combined to create a diffusely radiant yellow. The furniture was made in

the Lyle and Dumbach workshop, as were the hanging silk lanterns, which add a soft, romantic evening glow, facing.

Family hats, including a
mortarboard graduation cap,
bedeck a restored oak
hall tree original to the
house. The blue and white
"Tented Stripe" wallpaper
is a patriotic contrast to the
"Rectory Red" painted floors.
Needlepoint pillows are from
the 1960s.

John Lyle and Mark Umbach A Red, White and Blue Yankee in Maine

THE VICTORIAN cottage on a small island off the coast of Maine had originally been built at the turn of the twentieth century and had been lovingly cared for by family members for generations. But by the time John and Mark's clients, a gracious couple from the South, purchased the home as a northern retreat in 2005, it had passed through several hands and was being operated as a guesthouse. Subsequent owners had not been sympathetic to its past: floors had been carpeted with orange shag rayon, walls were nicotine-stained brown and the ceilings in several rooms were in advanced stages of collapse. Cafe curtains covered the windows, and the baths had mold and mildew.

The new owners were divided—the wife had dreams of a cozy cottage, while the husband was enamored of boathouses and the sea—so John and Mark cleverly created a cottage that appealed to husband and wife alike. A local builder was engaged and the home underwent a major facelift. A bead board ceiling was added in the living room and painted in high gloss "Dorset Cream." Farrow & Ball "Tented Stripe" paper in indigo and cream was applied to the walls, and the floors were covered in "Rectory Red" for a patriotic and nautical look. Accents such as a jade green sofa and armchairs along with family

THE LIVING ROOM

evokes the nautical in Yankee red, white and blue.
The newly added bead board ceiling is painted in high gloss "Dorset Cream." Walls are
papered with "Tented Stripe" in indigo and cream, and the floors are painted "Rectory Red"
(with an extra dash of pigment). A comfortable mix of
family antiques softens the strong colors and lends a lived-in cottage look.

antiques and heirlooms softened the room and helped create the desired cottage appeal. The adjacent sunroom was painted in "Pointing" white to emphasize its sun-washed crispness; furniture was upholstered with a bright floral cotton.

The kitchen was returned to its cottage origins with a diamond-patterned floor painted in "Cooking Apple Green" and "Pointing"; an original round claw-foot table and chairs were also updated with a fresh coat of "Pointing."

Upstairs, the guest bath was brightened with a claw-foot tub painted in vermillion red "Blazer" for a colorful contrast against the "Green Ground" walls. The narrow and winding hallway was papered with vintage sailboats in continuation of the nautical theme, and the master bedroom was stried in "Yellow Ground" and "Pointing" white for a sunny, traditional English look. "Tented Stripe" paper in a coordinating yellow extended to the adjacent small nursery under the eaves. "Pointing" in a guest bedroom, with a touch of "Dorset Cream," highlights a collection of red and white transferware plates hung on the wall.

Colorful, amusing and patriotic, the cottage has now become a much-loved Yankee retreat for this Southern couple.

upines grow wild on the island and are a favorite summertime flower. Here a vase of the royal purple flowers from a nearby field rest on the mantel painted in "Dorset Cream." Comfortable armchairs are upholstered in soft, jade green with an ecru welt for an inviting, informal cottage appeal, facing. ❧ The narrow stripes of a handwoven carpet in indigo and cream on the narrow staircase echo the similarly patterned "Tented Stripe" wallpaper, lending to the boathouse look, left.

THE MASTER BEDROOM IS

decorated in a strie of pale "Yellow Ground" and "Pointing" and is furnished with wicker

chairs for a comfortable and unpretentious cottage look, facing. ❧ The narrow

nooks and crannies of the upstairs hall are accented with a nautical paper of Yankee clipper ships;

woodwork is painted "Dorset Cream," above.

THE ADJOINING NURSERY

is papered in yellow "Tented Stripe," which emphasizes the sloped roofline

of the room, facing. ❧ An upstairs guest room under the eaves is painted in "Pointing" with a

touch of "Dorset Cream" to accent a collection of red and white

transferware plates. A red and white gingham bed skirt and red and white quilted matelasse

bed coverlet adds to the romantic look, above.

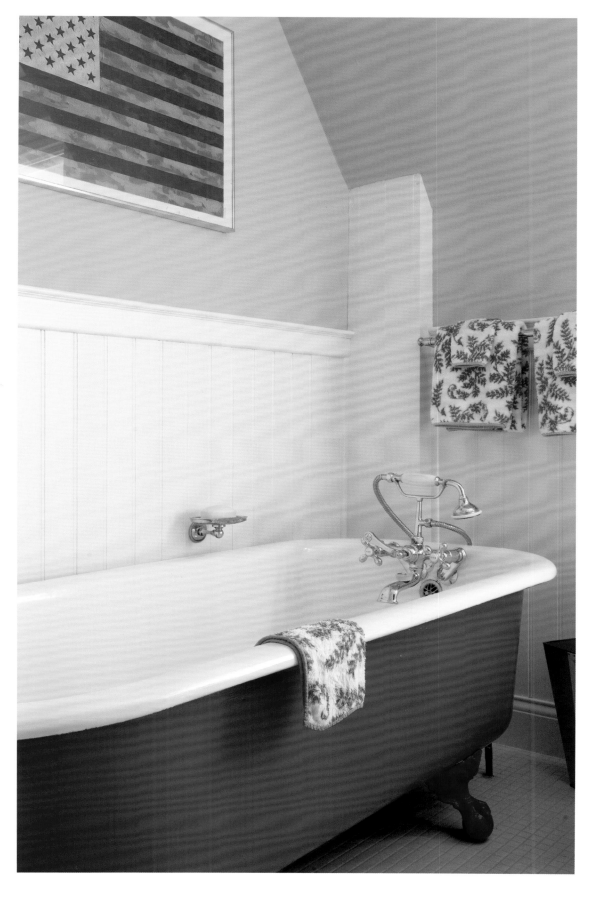

The original corner marble sink is accented against "Green Ground" walls in the guest bath, facing. The vintage-style medicine cabinet was added during restoration. ❧ A claw-foot tub painted in lively "Blazer" (the red color was inspired by the blazers worn by students at Cambridge).is the main feature of the guest bath. Woodwork is painted in "Pointing," right.

The dining room, which opens off the living room, is papered in nautical indigo blue and cream "Tented Stripe." The bead board ceiling is lightened with high gloss "Dorset Cream" and the floors are painted in rich "Rectory Red." The light-washed sunroom beyond is painted in white "Pointing," facing. An American country oak sideboard in the dining room holds a collection of antique brass candlesticks and bowls and is lit by a pair of Victorian tole lanterns. The stripes of "Tented Stripe" wallpaper add color and visual interest, right.

THE SUNROOM IS PAINTED

in "Pointing" to emphasize its fresh, sunny atmosphere. The nautical theme is continued
with room accents, facing. ✑ The kitchen is returned to its early-twentieth-century
charm, its floor painted in diamonds of "Cooking Apple Green" and "Pointing."
Woodwork is also painted in "Pointing," as are the oak table and chairs, which are original to
the house. A 1970s china cabinet holds apple green and cream dishware, above.

Creamy carnations and pale yellow roses
are accented against the embroidered fabric headboard
from Chelsea Editions and the yellow walls are
painted in "Dorset Cream," below. ℀ "Dorset Cream"
gives the master bedroom a warm
and inviting look. The molding adds further
architectural interest, facing.

SALLIE GIORDANO
TRADITION WITH A TWIST
ON PARK AVENUE

SALLIE GIORDANO was raised on the principles of good design—her mother Leta Austin Foster's name has been well known in interior design for many years. After attending the New York School of Design, Sallie followed in her mother's footsteps; she has headed the New York office of Leta Austin Foster since 1992, where projects range from city lofts to compounds on the beach. And while Sallie is versatile in a range of styles from classic European to the most modern, her forte is adding an unexpected twist to traditional design, as she has expertly demonstrated in a recent renovation at an enviable address: Park Avenue on the Upper East Side.

Since the seven rooms of the apartment had classic proportions but little in the way of architectural note, Sallie began by adding interest with classic paneling, sturdy mahogany doors and molding details that included overscaled trim work above the doors, which were relocated to allow for better traffic flow and furniture placement. Bookcases were built in to the dining room so it could double as a library, a popular treatment in space-starved New York.

While the husband preferred conventional treatments, the wife was more attracted to a

modern look, so Sallie gave the rooms a bit of a twist with unexpected ethnic fabrics and prints in the library and hand-painted stripes in the living room in Farrow & Balls "Clunch" and "Old White." The library was painted in "Matchstick," a neutral background for a collection of Hudson River School paintings and a fine complement to the color and verve of the Braquenie Indienne fabrics.

The master bedroom was painted in warm and comfortable "Dorset Cream," with added moldings and embroidered fabrics from Chelsea Editions lending an old-world charm to a formerly nondescript room.

$\mathcal{L}$eo, the family's border ter-
rier, enjoys playing catch in the
living room. Walls are hand
striped in Farrow & Ball
"Clunch" and "Old White" to
provide a pleasing backdrop for
a collection of traditional
European antiques. Claremont
"Rosa Bernal" printed linen
gives the upholstered sofa and
armchairs a note of color and
warmth, left. ❧ Architectural
details including mahogany
doors and commanding over-
door trim are highlighted
against the "Clunch" and "Old
White" hand-striped walls,
above right. ❧ Subtly striped
walls are a sophisticated and
unexpected touch, right.

THE LIBRARY, WHICH DOUBLES

as the dining room, is given architectural interest with moldings and built-in bookcases (not shown). Walls are painted "Matchstick" to provide a pleasing backdrop for paintings and unexpected Indian fabrics.

SALLIE GIORDANO
HISTORY REINTERPRETED IN RICHMOND, VIRGINIA

WHEN CLIENTS of Sallie and her mother, Leta Austin Foster, consulted them to restore Milburne, a historic home in Richmond, Virginia, Sallie knew exactly what was required: a freshening of the house for its current occupants, descendants of the original owners, but keeping in mind its illustrious past. Designed by well-known architect William Bottomley, it was completed in 1935 and is considered his finest work. Commissioned by Walter Robertson, head of the China Lobby, it was frequently used to entertain government leaders and heads of state, including Queen Elizabeth and Prince Philip, who stayed there on an American visit.

The Georgian Revival mansion was originally decorated in colors specified by Bottomley, ones closely matched today by Farrow & Ball's muted palette. Original pieces of furnishing also remained—from oriental rugs, a secretary in the living room, and the sideboard and overmantel mirror in the dining room, to canopy beds in the girls' bedroom—so Sallie began by carefully preserving those pieces and supplementing them with antiques and furnishings in the style of the original decor. Newly upholstered, comfortable seating and sophisticated Farrow & Ball colors helped bring the classic grace of Milburne forward into the twenty-first century.

The grand entry foyer—highlighted by a dramatic, sweeping staircase—was lightened with a mix of "All White" and "Pointing" on the woodwork and peaceful "Teresa's Green" on the dado beneath the chair rail molding. Baseboards were picked out in "Off-Black," which Bottomley had specified in his original plans. A staircase runner from Mark Carpets at Scalamandré in a complementary aqua blue-green carried color upstairs. Original details were carefully preserved, such as the overhead Chinoiserie lantern that was designed by Bottomley to coordinate with the fretwork in the balustrade. Antiques, including a pair of Swedish benches, were chosen to lend a fresh look that was also elegant and sophisticated.

The entry opens to the living room, which was also painted in the restful aqua tones of "Teresa's Green." The ornate plaster and woodwork was highlighted with chalky, stone-colored "Clunch" and baseboards were continued in "Off-Black." The painting above the fireplace is

In the living room, dramatic
floor-to-ceiling arched windows
overlook the nearby river and afford sweeping
vistas of the countryside. Woodwork
is painted in neutral "Clunch" and walls glow
with peaceful "Teresa's Green."

The dining room was papered in an *Aqua Floral Swag* from Mauny, and the woodwork, including a built-in niche, was painted in neutral *"Pointing."*

by Armfield, a well-known English genre painter and a relative of the current owners. The secretary was original to the house; furnishings were updated with chaises upholstered in damask accented with hand-embroidered pillows. The crystal sconces above the fireplace were also original. The dining room was papered in an aqua floral swag from Mauny, and the woodwork, including a built-in niche, was painted in neutral "Pointing." Plasterwork around the tops of the walls was in poor condition, damaged by previous applications of gold radiator paint; rather than attempting a complicated and costly replacement, it was simply restored in situ and painted with "Pointing," which successfully hides the repairs. The rug, dining table and overmantel mirror were all, fortunately, original to the room. Antique Chippendale chairs were found and covered in horse-

hair to complement the table. A painting of Jane Armfield, an ancestor of the owners, was hung over the fireplace.

The adjacent breakfast room was given a fresh lease on life by painting the woodwork vivid "Folly Green" to accent the wallpaper; a copy of the original from Mauny. Furnishings included the owner's mother's china displayed on the shelves. Bright color was continued into the butler's pantry, where the floors and cupboard interiors were painted in striking "Rectory Red," while the woodwork was made clean and fresh with "Pointing."

An extension of the main house is connected by an exterior screened loggia whose brick walls were painted in "Pointing" as well. A powder room was made warm and inviting with the dado painted toasty "Blazer" red; the woodwork is accented in "Pointing." An adjoining men's lounge was hung with Farrow & Ball "Melrose" wallpaper for a traditional look; the woodwork color is "Pointing."

Upstairs the master bedroom was kept cool and restful, the woodwork painted in "Green Stone" (a serene gray found in eighteenth-century paneled rooms) with accents of "Pointing." A beautiful painted bed from Julia Gray was highlighted with a hand-smocked half canopy and bed panels in sheer Swiss "Batiste" from Claremont. The girls' room still held the original twin canopy beds, which Sallie hung with cotton panels embroidered in France. Woodwork was painted "Green Blue" (which can read either green or blue, depending on what it is paired with) to coordinate with documentary wallpaper and drapes from Mauny. The nursery woodwork was painted in cheerful "Green Ground" (apple green) with "Pointing" accents. A rocking horse that belonged to the owners as a child, along with Raggedy Ann and Andy dolls, help give the room a storybook appeal.

THE DRAMATIC ENTRY

foyer focuses on a sweeping staircase.
Woodwork is painted in a combination of "All
White" and "Pointing" for a clean look,
while the dado beneath the
chair railing is painted "Teresa's Green,"
which complements the aqua tones of the wallpaper. Baseboards are picked
out in "Off-Black," as the original architect
specified. Antiques include
a French Bombay chest and a pair
of Swedish benches.

STUNNING WOOD AND PLASTERWORK

moldings and detailing are a highlight of the home. In the living room, stone-colored "Clunch" accents the trim work against the walls, which are painted "Teresa's Green," a pleasing aqua. The secretary is original to the house. Chairs and a sofa upholstered in damask provide comfortable seating, left. ❧ Fireplace detail shows the beautifully carved woodwork accented in "Clunch," above.

A built-in niche in the dining room is painted "Pointing" white to emphasize its handsome architectural detailing, top. ❧ Detail of the plasterwork in the dining room, which is painted in "Pointing." The plasterwork had been originally covered with gold radiator paint, and resulting damage was repaired in situ, above. ❧ The dining room is papered in a classic French design from Mauny, and the woodwork is picked out in "Pointing" (except for "Off-Black" baseboards). Original furnishings include the dining room table, sideboard and overmantel mirror, right.

Sunlight streams into the breakfast room, painted in vivid "Folly Green." Walls are papered in a reproduction of the original French wallpaper. A cheerful green and white "Eaton Check" from Colefax & Fowler is used to upholster the chair seats, facing. ✥ The owner's mother's china is displayed in the built-in breakfast room shelves. Woodwork is painted "Folly Green," a late-eighteenth-century neo-classical green that complements the French Mauny wallpaper, above left. ✥

The adjoining butler's pantry is enlivened with "Rectory Red" floors and cabinet interiors; the woodwork is painted with pleasant "Pointing." A vintage light fixture hangs overhead, above right. ✥

THE ADJOINING MEN'S LOUNGE

is papered in "Melrose" for a traditional look, with woodwork

accented in "Pointing." Antique French bamboo chairs are a handsome complement, facing.

❧ An exterior loggia is painted in eggshell emulsion "Pointing," while the dado inside

is enlivened with "Blazer" red, above.

In the master bedroom the woodwork is painted in calming "Green Stone" with "Pointing" accents. An antique French wallpaper from Mauny covers the walls. The bed from Julia Gray is accented with a hand-smocked half canopy of sheer Swiss Batiste from Claremont, and the sheets are hand embroidered from Leta Austin Foster, above. ✻ A fauteuil

in the master bedroom is glazed with "White Tie" for a look of period elegance, above right. ❧ The girls' room still has its original twin canopy beds, now upholstered in cotton panels custom embroidered in France. The woodwork is painted "Green Blue" to coordinate with the documentary French wallpaper from Mauny, below right.

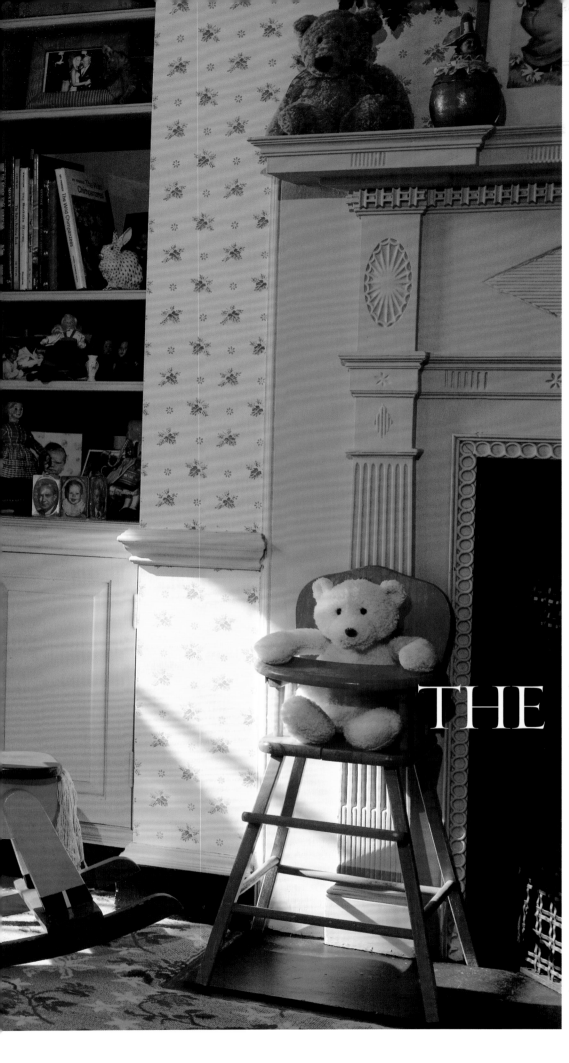

THE NURSERY

is straight from a storybook, with "Green Ground" woodwork accented in "Pointing" and pretty toile curtains from Claremont. Antique toys, including the owner's rocking horse, are now enjoyed by a new generation. The family's golden retriever, Virginia, enjoys a peaceful interlude while the children are away, left.

The striking entry
sets the tone for the house. The
woodwork painted in "Pointing"
was inspired from a historic plantation in Virginia. Walls are
striped with "Green Ground"
and "Pointing" to lighten the
mood of the home.
The antique walnut bench is covered in "Darien Check" from
Schumacher.

LETA AUSTIN FOSTER
DELRAY BEACH, FLORIDA, THIRTIES REVIVAL

LETA AUSTIN FOSTER is one of Palm Beach's best-known decorators. She also maintains offices in New York City and Los Angeles and has been designing interiors for thirty-five years. Her pop-ular Palm Beach boutique carries custom accessories from lamp shades to linens, with hand-embroidered bed sheets always in high demand. Well versed in any period style, Leta's hallmark is comfort—combining style and sophistication with ease of living. Leta con-siders an interior successful if it doesn't look decorated but rather has a timeless appeal, the product of good, classic design.

Delray Beach in southern Florida is one of the area's more historic communities, first founded by pineapple growers in the late-nineteenth century. Charming, palm-lined streets with homes from the twenties and thirties face the ocean, and it's easy to understand its continuing appeal. One of these his-toric homes built in the 1930s was purchased as a win-ter retreat by a couple from the mountains of Virginia. They wanted pretty and sunny interiors, light and airy yet comfortable for their children's and grandchildren's visits.

As the living and dining room opened onto each other, Leta applied the same wall treatment to both: trelliage panels painted in "Pointing" below the chair rail, with broad stripes of "Green Ground" and "Pointing" above in a dragged and ragged finish for

which overlooks the Intracoastal Waterway (a 1,200-mile sheltered route for boats along the eastern seaboard),

is light and sunny with walls painted in "White Tie" sponged over "Pointing." The wood ceiling is finished with "Pale Hound" in a water-based eggshell finish to

reflect the surrounding light, above. ❧ Well-coordinated color and detail are what make the garden room successful.

The ceiling is painted in "Pale Hound" eggshell finish and the walls are sponged in "White Tie" over "Pointing," facing inset.

visual interest and depth. The floors were bleached and stained in a large diamond pattern, with alternating squares of clear wood and "All White" to enliven the space and add movement.

A striking entry staircase with complementary trelliage railings painted in "Pointing" and walls striped with "Green Ground" and "Pointing" was inspired by Gunston Hall Plantation in Virginia. A sunny garden room overlooking the pool and the Intracoastal Waterway was kept light with walls painted in "White Tie" sponged over "Pointing," accented with a ceiling of "Pale Hound" applied in a water-based eggshell finish for a delicate sheen. Leta added matchstick blinds for privacy and protection from the midday sun.

The library was made warm and intimate with a hand-painted faux bois finish of sycamore created with "Straw" and "India Yellow." Leta's success is in her attention to details—she was even careful to choose just the right wastebasket from her accessories collection for the room.

The upstairs master bedroom was kept airy and comfortable with wallpaper from Nina Campbell and matchstick blinds lightened with "Pointing," which was also used for the molding and trim. Leta designed a Chinoiserie chandelier to coordinate with a Julia Gray bed and painted it "Eating Room Red" with gold leaf.

The painted diamond floors were continued to the upstairs guest wing, where one of the rooms was covered with pale stripes of "Dayroom Yellow" and "Pointing." Contrasted against the aged-looking "Minster Green" painted floor, the room has a charming cottage appeal.

The master bedroom beckons like a secluded, wooded bower with a soothing green and taupe palette. The matchstick blinds and woodwork were repainted in "Pointing." The Chinoiserie-style four-poster bed from Julia Gray is accented overhead with a chandelier made by Leta's workroom and painted in "Eating Room Red" and gold leaf. Curtains and the duvet cover are constructed with Colefax & Fowler's "Boxwood," adding to the garden appeal, left. ✵ Painted faux finishes are continued upstairs in the guest wing. The doors are grained in "Straw" and "India Yellow" and the floor is painted in "Pointing" diamonds. The guest room walls are covered in pale stripes of "Dayroom Yellow" and "Pointing," and the floor in "Minster Green" reinforces the feel of a cozy seaside cottage, above.

THE LIBRARY WALL AND DOORS

are faux bois, painted in "Straw" and "India Yellow." Furnishings include an
English Regency chair upholstered in a playful Colefax & Fowler fabric, above. ❧ The library is
faux bois painted in a sycamore grain using "Straw" and "India Yellow." The ceiling is a
complementary, cool "Hound Lemon," a favorite of John Fowler. Leta chose every detail carefully,
including the amusing wastebasket from her accessories collection, facing.

The living room is furnished with a mix of French and
English Regency antiques and comfortable seating. Walls are hand-striped with "Green Ground"
and "Pointing" above a trelliaged dado painted in "Pointing," which is also used for the mantel. The linen chenille vel-
vet rug was custom made by Stark to coordinate with the light green and cream palette of the room.
Note the hand-painted accent pillow from Leta's workroom on the sofa, above. 🎨 The hand-painted floor in a pattern of diamonds carries through in the dining room, which also
features an Italian-inspired mural on the wall, facing.

Leta Austin Foster
Hobe Sound, Florida, British Colonial Retreat

HOBE SOUND is one of southern Florida's most scenic communities, with white, sandy beaches and rivers with an abundance of wildlife, from playful porpoises to gentle manatees. The owners of this home, sited directly on the ocean, had built it in the 1960s. Leta helped them freshen the interiors with the theme of a Colonial British retreat. The views of the ocean became the focal point in the living room, where the walls were painted with large (seven-inch) stripes of "Tallow," a warm off-white, and "Pointing." A sand-colored sisal rug from Stark Carpet continued the beach theme indoors, as did the extensive use of shells. In the library the walls were grain-painted in a blend of "Ringwold Ground" and "New White," for the cozy and inviting look of a gentlemen's club.

"Pale Powder" (a pale powder blue) on the ceiling brought the sea inside, and comfortable, custom-made furniture was upholstered in a colorful Pierre Frey fabric, "Enchantee," fit for a Raj. The master bedroom—a large, cavernous room—was made more intimate with the addition of molding and paneling, which was painted with "Pointing" in an eggshell finish. Color was introduced with the owners' Delftware collection in soft yellows and blues, which Leta accented with selected antiques such as lamps made from Scottish candlesticks. The powder room cabinetry was painted in "Green Ground" for a pleasing accent to the stylized floral "Anna-Maria" wallpaper from George Spencer.

THE LIBRARY IS GRAIN-PAINTED

with "Ringwold Ground" and "New White" for intimacy and accented with a pale sea-blue ceiling of "Pale Powder." Custom-made furniture is upholstered with a colorful glazed linen, left. ❧ A nineteenth-century English drinks table is ready for cocktails with a pair of crystal decanters from the owners' collection. The walls are faux-grained in "Ringwold Ground" and "New White," above.

THE POWDER ROOM IS PAPERED

in "Anna-Maria" from George Spencer, while the "Green Ground" cabinets provide
a pleasing accent, above. ❧ An antique mirror reflects the upholstered headboard in the master
bedroom, which is enhanced with molding and paneling painted in
"Pointing" eggshell. The lamps are made from antique Scottish candlesticks. The lamp shades
and headboard are upholstered with the floral blue cotton
print "Herbier," from Clarence House, facing.

Leta Austin Foster
Caribbean Treasure on Jupiter Island, Florida

JUPITER ISLAND is one of the most desirable locations in southern Florida. The southernmost of Florida's three Barrier Islands, located off West Palm Beach, it has been a favorite for treasure seekers since 1715, when the Spanish Plata Fleet wrecked off the coast, spewing their cargo of silver and gold coins onto the beaches (they still turn up in the sand today). The owners of this comfortable oceanside home wanted a Caribbean Island–style décor, and so Leta blended soft ocean colors of light blue water with pale sand, highlighting the owners' collection of Chinese export furniture, including a striking screen. Walls in the large living room were painted in Farrow & Ball "Pale Powder," a soft sea blue, while the woodwork on the tall, arched French door opening onto the ocean was accented in "Pointing."

Furnished with a mix of antiques, a pair of Billy Baldwin–style chairs and other custom furniture from Leta's workshop, the room is color-ful, inviting and personal. A long central hall runs the length of the house and, in tropical fashion, opens off to the other rooms in the house. Walls were painted in "Pale Powder" and "Farrow's Cream" to bring the seaside indoors; the woodwork was contrasted with neutral "Pointing." The theme of the outdoors was continued in the master bedroom, which overlooks the ocean as well. Airy Swiss tambour curtains were hung on the windows to mitigate the glare while allowing light to fill the room. Chelsea Edition's "Large Check" in sea foam was used for the main curtains, and chair upholstery highlights the aqua blue of the sea. Woodwork was painted in "Pointing" for a neutral background. A folding corner screen and small chest were painted Swedish style in "Pale Powder," "Pointing" and "Clunch" for nautical accents.

R ooms open off the central hall, which runs the length of the house. Walls are painted in "Pale Powder" and "Farrow's Cream" to bring the colors of the beach indoors. Woodwork is painted in "Pointing," above. ❧ The spacious living room overlooks the oceanfront, which is brought indoors with walls of airy blue "Pale Powder" and woodwork in soft "Pointing," right.

THE COLORS OF
THE GARDEN
AND OCEAN

waves beyond are brought into the master
bedroom with curtains and upholstery in
"Large Check" from Chelsea Editions in sea
foam green. Woodwork is painted in neutral "Pointing," and a folding corner screen
and side table are Swedish-painted with
"Pale Powder," "Pointing" and "Clunch."

Detail of the delicately painted sky above the bed, with the paneling painted in "Pale Powder," "Clunch" and "New White." An antique French tole chandelier accents the space, left. ❧ The master bedroom of this spec house is personalized with upholstered walls and paneling highlighted in "Pale Powder," "Clunch" and "New White," facing.

Leta Austin Foster
Spec House Magic in South Florida

WHEN THE OWNERS of this speculation-built house in a southern Florida subdivision contacted Leta, they explained they had bought the house so their daughter could ride in the southern Florida horse shows season. Meant for only a few months of occupancy each year, the owners wanted Leta to make the house less of a standard tract home and imbue it with some much-needed individuality. In the master bedroom, Leta accomplished this with paint and color. Paneling was picked out in "Pale Powder" and "Clunch," which were highlighted against the "New White" walls. An airy floral cotton from Bennison Fabrics was applied to the walls, headboard and chairs. A delicate sky mural was hand-painted on the ceiling to add another personal touch.

The master bedroom
is light and pleasing with woodwork and
paneling painted in "Pointing," which is also employed
to lighten and antique the formerly dark
wooden bed. The embroidered matelasse is from
Leta Austin Foster Boutique.

LETA AUSTIN FOSTER
GEORGIAN REVIVAL IN
SAINT LOUIS

DECORATING A CLASSIC thirties Georgian Revival home for clients in St. Louis was very much a family affair, as Leta had designed interiors for their parents and siblings as well. When the owners, a young couple, contacted Leta, they asked her to update the traditional home and give it a younger feeling but with a respect for its past. Leta chose a simple and welcoming palette of light colors: "Pointing" in the living and family rooms, and a blend of pale blue "Borrowed Light" and natural wood stain on the kitchen woodwork for a sunlit Provençal appeal. The master bedroom was given more visual interest with applied panels painted in "Pointing," and the adjoining master bath was striped with hand-painted bands of "Teresa's Green" and "Pointing."

THE MASTER BEDROOM HAS MORE INTEREST

with moldings applied to simulate paneling and painted with straightforward "Pointing." The mantel is also painted with "Pointing." Scalamandré "Brompton Check" enlivens two chairs that coordinate nicely with the aqua and white patterned carpet from Prosource, left. ✺ The master bath is fresh with stripes of "Teresa's Green" and "Pointing" on the walls and the cabinetry is bright with "Pointing," above.

THE KITCHEN, ADJOINING THE

family room, is given a cheerful and airy French Provençal appeal with woodwork

treated in a combination of pale blue "Borrowed Light" and wood stain.

Walls are "Pointing" white, facing and above.

The family room walls are painted in "Pointing," and "Les Nids," a child-friendly Claremont fabric in a small blue check, gives the room a lighthearted feeling of fun, facing. ❧ The family's golden retriever relaxes in the living room as morning sunlight streams in the windows. Walls are painted in "Pointing" to lighten the room and retain its classic style. Chelsea Edition's "Large Check" is the uphol-stery selection, and a Stark sisal carpet helps make the room less serious, above. ❧ The embroidered white linen curtains from Chelsea Editions are complemented by the simple white "Pointing" wall color, left.

La Jolie Lulu, the owner's Bichon Frise,
strikes a meditative pose beneath the calfskin-topped oak bar
inspired by French designer Dupre Lafon. Ed Ruscha's *Legs* hangs above. Wall
and ceiling are painted with "Clunch," a warm backdrop for the
artwork and antiques, including a trio of nineteenth-century rock crystal
obelisks, below. ❧ Sunlight streams into the light and airy living room, facing.
Furnishings are an eclectic mix of old and new, including a nineteenth-century
Buddha from the estate of Peggy Ward, a 1940s bronze
and ostrich leather stool, and an antique Oushak carpet.

Kim Alexandriuk
Traditional Tudor
Update in Los Angeles

KIM ALEXANDRIUK is a unique and upcoming designer. Raised in Berlin, she obtained degrees in fine art and economics from the Universite de Lyons in France and trained at the Getty Conservation Institute before entering the field of interior design. Kim likes to draw on her European roots, combining a reverence for architecture with classic design and color to emote both warmth and a sense of timelessness.

When she first met her client in Los Angeles, Kim found the home was a traditional 1940s Tudor, dark and uninviting, with small, closed rooms and narrow, gloomy hallways. Her goal was to preserve a sense of the home's history and at the same time bringing it into the present, embracing the beautiful climate of southern California. Kim changed the flow of the rooms to allow for easier circulation and brought the outdoors inside by adding larger windows and several sets of French doors opening to the back gardens. An inviting sunroom was designed at the back of the house with a large picture window looking onto the backyard fountain and lavender hedges; the window was positioned to be seen from the front door, thus creating an enchanting vista of the garden upon entering the home.

The dining room is centered on a Bohemian crystal chandelier handmade in France. Walls and ceiling are painted in Farrow & Ball "Slipper Satin," a neutral background for John Baldessari's *Woman Looking at Plants (With Two Carrots)*.

The dining room walls and ceiling were painted with subtle *"Slipper Satin"* to highlight striking artwork and a Bohemian crystal chandelier. The living room was painted in Farrow & Ball café au lait *"Clunch."*

Crown moldings, baseboards and stair rails were changed and paneling added in the master bath. The woodwork throughout the house was painted Farrow & Ball "All White" for a fresh, clean look. Calm palettes were chosen for the rooms to bring light inside and enhance the owner's important collections of modern art and photographs. The dining room walls and ceiling were painted with subtle "Slipper Satin" to highlight striking artwork and a Bohemian crystal chandelier. The living room was painted in Farrow & Ball café au lait "Clunch."

The owner enjoys cooking and entertaining, so the kitchen was transformed into a warm and welcoming space by finishing the custom oak cabinetry with Farrow & Ball "Rectory Red" and then staining it with a deep brown glaze that was partially rubbed off to show the grain of the wood. Creamy "Dimity" was chosen for the ceiling and walls in the master bath and bedroom to provide a suitable background for striking photography by Edward Boubat, William Klein and other important photographers. A small powder room off the main entrance was treated as a separate jewel box, with walls custom stried in "Clunch" with an overcoat of "French Gray." "Clunch" was used again in the family room as a sophisticated background for Oriental and modern art.

Light, airy and inviting, the house has been transformed into an open and sun-filled home reflective of the owner and its beautiful southern California setting.

MULTI-HUED FIESTA WARE ECHOES

the warmth and color of the custom oak kitchen cabinets painted "Rectory Red" and overglazed with brown.
The blacksplash, a stainless steel tile from Rhomboid Sax, provides a modern contrast, facing. ❧ Jim Shaw's *Dream Object*
rests on the counter near the sink. Walls and ceiling are painted with Farrow & Ball "Shaded White," above.

"DIMITY" WAS CHOSEN FOR THE WALLS

and ceiling in the master bath, which is decorated with photographs
by Edward Boubat, William Klein, Willy Ronis and Robert Doisneau. The Italian engraved
terra-cotta floor pavers pick up the warm tones of the creamy walls. Wainscoting
painted "All White" lends architectural interest and nicely complements the warm
color of the "Dimity" walls, above and facing.

T he master bedroom walls and ceiling are painted with "Dimity" to create a subtle and serene environment. A custom walnut table with faux shagreen top flanks a custom-made steel canopy bed. The bedside table lamp of Murano glass is from the 1950s, facing. ✥ The fireplace in the master bedroom is simply "All White." The tones of the c. 1920 Italian alabaster box on the mantel complement the colors of the walls, right.

The downstairs powder room becomes a jewel box, its walls painted with a custom strie in "Clunch" with an overcoat of "French Gray." The wainscoting of warm, Italian terrazzo echoes the colors of the upper walls. A custom-designed Jacques Quinet–style commode and c. 1920 French crystal chandelier and sconces add to the opulent look, above. ❦ Bauhaus mirror c. 1920 reflects a photograph of Picasso by Brassai. The soft tones of "Clunch" stried on the walls and overcoated with "French Gray" complement the vintage furnishings, left. ❦ The family room, facing, created from two smaller rooms, opens to the back garden with French doors. The walls and ceiling are painted with "Clunch," a warm and inviting backdrop for the owner's collection of art and antiques. A 1950s French bronze marble-topped coffee table rests on a c. 1880 Mahal carpet. The sofa was custom designed and complements the c. 1920 Anglo-Indian chair. A French mirrored obelisk lamp c. 1930 reflects the light from the garden back into the room.

JANEY JORDAN SMITH
CAPITOL HILL COLOR IN WASHINGTON, D.C.

JANEY JORDAN SMITH has always been appreciative of art and good design. Growing up in a small town in Central Texas provided her with a warm and nurturing childhood, one in which the arts were explored by the whole family. Janey remembers the excitement she felt looking through each new issue of *Architectural Digest* and the fun she would have trying to draw out floor plans for the homes. After studying interior design at the University of Texas at Austin, she spent a year in Tuscany. It's no surprise that the places she has visited find their way into her interiors, whether it's Italy, Sweden, France or England. Since making Washington, D.C., her home, Janey has enjoyed working on historic Capitol Hill and has learned to appreciate the charm and challenges of its late-nineteenth-century homes. Janey explains that she likes to create comfortable yet classic spaces, interiors that reflect her clients' tastes and achieve a balance of old and new by blend-

ing rich textures and interesting architectural details with intensely pigmented colors.

Janey had had her eye on the stately Georgian on the corner of her neighborhood for some time. One of Capitol Hill Historic District's few remaining completely detached homes, it had been sadly neglected. Janey was excited when the house was purchased in 2000 and a major restoration was begun, bringing the stately residence back to its former elegance and beauty. And she was thrilled when the new owners contacted her to help with the interiors, as they had been captivated by the Farrow & Ball colors she had used on another, nearby Capitol Hill project.

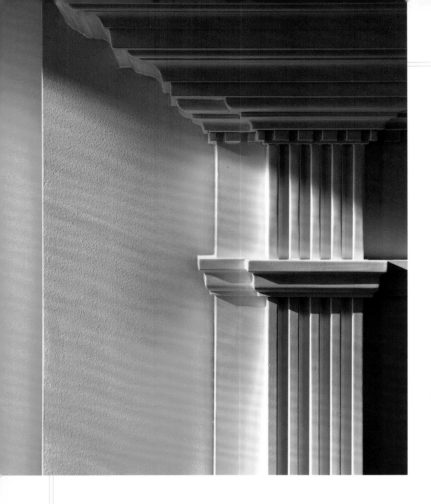

Sunlight streams into the living
room, highlighting the "Ciara Yellow" walls and "Citron" mantel, left.
❧ Hannibal, the family's Chesapeake Bay retriever, waits patiently
outside the dining room, which is painted in
Farrow & Ball "Eating Room Red," facing.

The house had an illustrious past, having been built in 1876 by James W. Whelpley and his wife Louisa. Mr. Whelpley was the assistant treasurer of the United States under President Grover Cleveland. By the time Janey's clients purchased the home, it had been converted into nine apartments and was jokingly referred to as the old "haunted mansion." The new owners have an active family of four energetic young boys and were attracted by the spaciousness of the home, its distinct, historic character and the large corner lot—a treat in the compact urban neighborhood.

Renovation took two years and was considerable. The house was completely gutted, leaving only the exterior brick walls, the center hall stud walls, the center staircase and sections of the flooring. A valuable resource for the restoration proved to be the great-granddaughter of Mr. Whelpley, who lived nearby and was able to provide photographs of the origi-

nal home that helped especially in the replacement of missing exterior details.

Color was the most important item on Janey's clients' list. The home's generous, sun-filled rooms were perfect for their large works of art brought from their previous home, a loftlike space, and the color in the artwork was used to guide the scheme for this home: warm Tuscan yellows, persimmon reds and subtle gray-greens. Farrow and Ball's historic colors seemed to have been made for the project.

Farrow & Ball "Lime White" was used as a neutral color to connect the three main levels of the home. The home is often a gathering space for friends and family, and it was important to the clients that the interior spaces reflect a welcoming spirit. Thus, the colors on the main level, "Citron," "Ciara Yellow" and "Eating Room Red," were chosen to create warm and inviting spaces. These colors then became the foundation for custom window treatments, furniture and unique lighting.

None of the home's four fireplace surrounds were salvageable, and so Janey created drawings for each and had them handcrafted. The dining room mantel was carefully constructed and aged with a distressed, old pine finish to complement the antique pine French refectory table from New Orleans that had been chosen for the dining table. Dining room walls were painted in Farrow & Ball "Eating Room Red," a most appropriate color for this family, who are well known for their culinary talents.

"Citron" and "Ciara Yellow" were chosen for the living room to emphasize the sunny, light-filled space. Tall, custom window treatments were created with natural tortoise shades and simple panels made from a silk stripe in complementary reds, greens and golds to allow light to stream in but also provide a measure of privacy. Filled with the family's collection of art, the room is now warm and inviting, even on the coldest of Washington's winter evenings.

Chester, the owners' golden Lab,

enjoys the cool Quebec limestone floors. Spaces throughout

the home were kept as open as possible. The dining room flows into the

central atrium and entry foyer beyond and is centered on

a custom cherry dining room table lit by Flos overhead hanging lamps.

Walls are painted in "Pointing."

Andre D'Elia
Toronto Reinterpreted

A TORONTO native, Andre D'Elia received his professional architecture degree from Carleton University in 1993. He opened his own firm, Superkul, Inc., in 2002 and has won numerous awards, including *Canadian Interiors*'s Best of Canada Award for St. Joseph Media in 2005. Andre likes to emphasize natural light, proportions and interior and exterior spaces and their relationships in his work.

Toronto is known for its neighborhoods of gracious older homes. When longtime residents of one of these historic districts decided to retire, they knew they wanted to remain in the same locale, a tree-lined boulevard of picturesque, early-twentieth-century homes, where they had lived for thirty years. So, working with D'Elia, they did just that, subdividing their generous lot and designing a refreshingly modern home that was quite a departure from their Tudor Revival and yet would knit seamlessly into the conventional fabric of their neighborhood. To achieve this, D'Elia used proportions and materials for the new house based on cues from the established neighbors. Existing materials were reinterpreted: the use of red brick and dark window

frames echoed those on the surrounding homes, while a cantilevered canopy, parapets, sill and head heights were all designed to be proportionate to and reminiscent of the other facades on the street.

The house was built with two principal volumes: a lower, two-story brick and wood box that wraps around a higher, two-and-one-half-story volume in the center. Topped by a glazed lantern, this central space provides the ordering element of the house, allowing light to reach deep inside the middle core of the home. Rooms are organized around this central volume, and motorized vents in the lantern allow for passive convective cooling and ventilation.

Interior finishes emphasize the interplay of space and volume: sandblasted Quebec limestone on the ground-level flooring, cherry wood millwork with stainless steel detailing throughout, clear maple hardwood floors upstairs, and clean and classic Farrow & Ball paints ("All-White," "Pointing," "Chemise," "Skylight" and "Mahogany"). Simple furnishings allow the strong architecture of the home to be the principal decoration.

THE LIVING ROOM

and dining room walls are
covered by Farrow & Ball "Pointing."
"Chemise," a subtle gray, was chosen for
the central elevator shaft.
Ceilings and trim are painted in neutral "All
White." Note the custom
cherry millwork highlighted by the cool color
palette. A Benson sofa rests
in the foreground.

A TWO-STORY ATRIUM

A two-story atrium fills the center of the house and lets light stream
down inside. A peaceful combination of "Chemise" on the central elevator shaft and "Pointing" on
the walls lets the architecture speak. Lighting fixtures were custom designed
by Lighting by Nelson & Garrett, Inc., facing. ❦ The stairs are clad in sandblasted Quebec
limestone. All metalwork, including the handrails and stringers, are
finished in Farrow & Ball "Mahogany," above.

Ray Brittain examines wallpaper being printed with blocks.

GLOSSARY OF FARROW & BALL COLORS
Color is what makes Farrow & Ball special. Here are color definitions and suggestions for their use.

LIME WHITE No.1
Neutral. No date, simply the color of untinted brightest white limewash or soft distemper.

HOUND LEMON® No.2
Neutral/Cool. Best used in well-lit spaces. This is a John Fowler color.

OFF-WHITE No.3
Neutral. This is a bright non-colored white. Use in place of brilliant white. Paler than No. 4 Old White with which it could be used as a picking-out color.

OLD WHITE No.4
Neutral. This color will look white in almost any "old" situation.

HARDWICK WHITE® No.5
Neutral. The colorway used to touch up old white limewash at Hardwick Hall. Probably not thought of as white except in large areas or with dark strong colors.

LONDON STONE No.6
Warm. John Sutcliffe's color taken from a Nash house in Regent's Park.

OCTAGON YELLOW® No.7
To match the color of the Octagon at the Bath Assembly Rooms as repainted in 1990.

STRING® No.8
Warm/Neutral. One of a series of pale earth pigment based colors which have been in continuous use either as an off-white with brighter colors or as its own color with a brighter white.

LIGHT STONE No.9
Warm. Cooler than No. 44 Cream. A traditional color that approximates to a very pale limestone.

FAWN No.10
Warm. An often-quoted color in eighteenth- and nineteenth-century decorating accounts for both walls and woodwork.

STONE WHITE No.11
Cool. Cooler again, but still not specifically colored. A "Palladian" color.

GREEN STONE No.12
Cool. As used in early-eighteenth-century paneled rooms.

OLIVE No.13
Cool. As used in early-eighteenth-century paneled rooms. A true earth green.

BERRINGTON BLUE® No.14
Though not visible now, based on scrapes and cross sections of the original boudoir scheme at Berrington Hall.

BONE® No.15
Cool. As woodwork or to simulate palest stone. Very good with the richness of some wallpapers.

CORD® No.16
A lively warm color to put with natural materials.

LIGHT GRAY No.17
Neutral. As a stone by itself or would appear white if used with, for example, No. 56 Etruscan Red.

FRENCH GRAY No.18
As the name suggests, also much used in nineteenth-century wallpapers.

Wallpaper rolls.

LICHEN No.19
Quieter and subtler than No. 13 Olive, for well lit rooms.

BUFF No.20
Here most close to its nineteenth-century color. Good with Victorian red schemes.

OINTMENT PINK® No.21
Based on scrapes and cross-sections taken in a number of houses and dating to the early years of the nineteenth century. Found in the dining room at Calke Abbey and the library at Kedleston . . . and yes, similar to the Regency scheme in the entrance hall and staircase at Castle Coole.

LIGHT BLUE No.22
Neutral. All color cards must surely include a light blue, but it is one of the peculiarities of the color blue to build up in intensity when painted in a room. If you wish for a slightly light blue room this, rather than the more obviously blue blues, is the one to try.

POWDER BLUE No.23
Taken from a sample color by John Fowler.

BALLROOM BLUE® No.24
Neither this nor No. 22 Light Blue or No. 23 Powder Blue are cold blues.

PIGEON® No.25
Based on late eighteenth- and nineteenth-century paint sections.

DOWN PIPE No.26
A color appropriate to imitate lead on exterior ironwork and to help "lose" plumbing against brickwork.

PARMA GRAY® No.27
John Fowler's name and color sample, though surely based on 1830s and 1840s schemes.

DEAD SALMON® No.28
The name comes from a painting bill for the library at Kedleston of 1805, though in fact analysis suggests that the color is far closer to No. 21 Ointment Pink®. Dead Salmon® as depicted here is rather more "tired" in character than it once was.

SUGAR BAG LIGHT® No.29
This is the color of Sugar Bag Blue which has bleached in the sun. It is also very like the blue of paper used for lining drawers in the late eighteenth century.

HAGUE BLUE® No.30
A strong blue, reminiscent of Dutch external woodwork.

RAILINGS No.31
A dark bronze color, suitable for exterior ironwork in place of the usual black.

COOKING APPLE GREEN® No.32
An old fashioned non-strongly colored green made from common earth pigments and lamp black rather than the newly developed nineteenth-century chemical pigments.

PEA GREEN No.33
A name often referred to in eighteenth-century accounts and here displayed as a clear green, as found on the original plain green paper of the Caricature Room at Calke Abbey.

CALKE GREEN® No.34
This is a color based directly on a cleaned version of the breakfast room at Calke Abbey.

MAHOGANY No.36
A standard and very useful color as used to imitate mahogany both internally and externally and in place of graining. An example of this color exists today on the doors in the Marble Hall at Kedleston.

" Plain Stripe" wallpaper is produced on the trough line.

HAY No.37

A bright but not excessively "hot" yellow. An early-nineteenth-century color.

BISCUIT No.38

Nearly a Bath Stone color. A sort of dark cream color used to suggest stone.

FOWLER PINK® No.39

A color John Fowler often used for paints and wallpapers, invariably used as a glaze.

MOUSE'S BACK® No.40

A quiet, neutral dark stone or drab color. Not to be recommended for use with white but very useful as an early-eighteenth-century color.

DRAB No.41

A typical early-eighteenth-century color. Good for both internal and external joinery.

PICTURE GALLERY RED® No.42

Based on the Picture Gallery at Attingham Park, but much cleaner and as a solid color not a varnished color.

EATING ROOM RED® No.43

A deep red, popular around the middle of the nineteenth century and made possible with the discovery of new pigments. It is related to red damask colorings.

CREAM No.44

A standard for any color card and based only on the addition of yellow ochre and, in this case, a little lamp black.

SAND No.45

Italian in origin. A common earth pigment based color.

GREEN SMOKE® No.47

An uncertain green/blue/grey color popular in the second half of the nineteenth century.

FOX RED® No.48

One of the clearest reds possible using finest burnt-earth pigments.

PORPHYRY PINK® No.49

This color was often used on walls as a foil to porphyry details such as columns during the Regency period.

BOOK ROOM RED® No.50

To do the work of either No. 42 Picture Gallery Red® or No. 43 Eating Room Red,® but in smaller rooms.

INDIA YELLOW No.66

First available in England in the eighteenth century, this pigment was produced by reducing the bright yellow urine of cows fed on a special diet of mango leaves.

FARROW'S CREAM® No.67

Farrow & Ball's original cream.

DORSET CREAM® No.68

A darker and more yellow version of No. 67 Farrow's Cream®.

PRINT ROOM YELLOW® No.69

Farrow & Ball mixed this color for an early restoration of an eighteenth-century print room.

ORANGERY No.70

Typical eighteenth-century terra-cotta color much used in orangeries.

PALE HOUND® No.71

For the effect of No. 2 Hound Lemon® when used in smaller rooms.

James Braitwaite checks quality control as raw materials are received.

GERVASE YELLOW® No.72

In memory of Gervase Jackson-Stops, the late advisor on architecture to the National Trust.

CIARA YELLOW® No.73

A typical bright Irish yellow as ordered for a project in County Cork.

CITRON No.74

A nineteenth-century trade name for a strong fairly acid yellow.

BALL GREEN® No.75

An old-fashioned distemper color from the archives.

FOLLY GREEN® No.76

A late-eighteenth-century neoclassical green, somewhat paler than the fashionable No. 33 Pea Green.

SUTCLIFFE GREEN® No.78

Connoisseurs often cite green as being the ultimate color to hang pictures on. This is a good alternative to No. 42 Picture Gallery Red®.

CARD ROOM GREEN® No.79

For those who think this color too drab, try with No. 10 Fawn.

SAXON GREEN® No.80

An early pre-British Standard color found on paintmakers' cards.

BREAKFAST ROOM GREEN® No.81

This color is lively both by day and candlelight.

DIX BLUE® No.82

A cleaner version of No. 23 Powder Blue.

CHAPPELL GREEN® No.83

This color will at times read green, at other times blue, depending on what colors are put with it.

GREEN BLUE No.84

Or should it be Blue Green? See explanation of No.83 Chappell Green®.

OVAL ROOM BLUE® No.85

A typical late-eighteenth-, early-nineteenth-century color that appears time and again in paint analysis. A lighter version of No.14 Berrington Blue®.

STONE BLUE® No.86

Indigo, as imported in the eighteenth century, came in lumps and was often known as "stone blue." This was a distemper color.

LAMP ROOM GRAY® No.88

A match to the original white which had dirtied down due to the trimming of lamp wicks. See also No. 5 Hardwick White®.

LULWORTH BLUE® No.89

A much used archive color named by Norman Chappell of Farrow & Ball.

CHINESE BLUE® No.90

Originally mixed for an eighteenth-century room displaying blue and white Chinese pots.

BLUE GRAY No.91

Try to view this color in isolation from the others.

CASTLE GRAY® No.92

First used on the exterior woodwork of a stone castle. A good period green for exterior use.

STUDIO GREEN® No.93

The best very dark colors often appear black on color cards and only show their color when painted on larger areas.

CARRIAGE GREEN No.94

This is a smart, bright, what we call "front door" dark green.

The wash area for the "Plain Stripe" wallpaper trough and tools has a beauty of its own.

BLACK BLUE No.95
This color is definitely blue when painted in large areas. It is a blue version of No. 93 Studio Green®.

RADICCHIO® No.96
A cleaner, less aged version of No. 43 Eating Room Red®. This is a strong red tempered by magenta.

SHADED WHITE No.201
Neutral. Just darker than No. 3 Off-White and lighter than No. 4 Old White. This can also be used as a light "drab" color.

PINK GROUND® No.202
The lightest red of our wallpaper ground colors.

TALLOW® No.203
Warm. A light off-white with a yellow tint.

PALE POWDER No.204
A pale, less colored version of No. 23 Powder Blue.

SKYLIGHT No.205
A definite light blue, lighter and cleaner than No. 22 Light Blue.

GREEN GROUND No.206
One of our wallpaper ground colors based on No. 32 Cooking Apple Green®.

RINGWOLD GROUND® No.208
Warm. An off-white color similar to No. 3 Off-White but with greater warmth.

BLUE GROUND® No.210
A blue wallpaper ground first used in our Damask collection.

STONY GROUND® No.211
A beige colored wallpaper ground color.

BLAZER® No.212
A bright vermillion red similar to the color of the sports blazer worn at St. John's College, Cambridge.

SAVAGE GROUND® No.213
A wallpaper ground color favored by Dennis Savage, a block printer par excellence.

ARSENIC® No.214
A green verdigris wallpaper ground color first used on our Napoleonic Bee wallpaper.

RECTORY RED® No.217
Vermillion, as in No. 212 Blazer® red, was often made cheaper by the addition of red lead which blackens with age, so changing the color to Rectory Red.

YELLOW GROUND No.218
One of our yellow wallpaper ground colors.

PITCH BLUE® No.220
A strong definite blue made warm by the addition of magenta.

BRINJAL® No.222
Often requested for interior walls as aubergine. This color originated as a nineteenth-century estate color.

BABOUCHE® No.223
The brightness of this yellow will intensify on large areas, so best try in situ with a sample pot.

Stainers are added to large vats of paint to produce individual colors.

MINSTER GREEN® No.224

An aged darkened version of No. 34 Calke Green®.

JOA'S WHITE® No.226

Warm. For devotees of No. 3 Off-White, Joa's White®, though just darker, has none of the coolness or perceived greenish nature of No. 3 Off-White.

ARCHIVE® No.227

Warm. Just darker and warmer than No. 226 Joa's White®, this color would normally be seen as a buff and not an off-white unless used with strong dark colors.

CORNFORTH WHITE® No.228

Neutral/Cool. In memory of John Cornforth, architectural historian and author of the landmark publication "English Decoration in the Eighteenth Century" and a friend to the historic interior, who guided the working lives of so many involved in their decoration. John was foremost in the 1970s and 1980s in reviving the Georgian palette of off-whites, stones, drabs and buffs.

ELEPHANT'S BREATH No.229

Warm/Neutral. A personal match for this famously named color by John Fowler. Some color experts believe it should be darker and more "slimy" in color! Use as a color in its own right, or as part of a "stone" scheme.

CALAMINE® No.230

Pinks do not always sit readily in the Farrow & Ball palette yet colors like this one appeared regularly in country house anterooms and boudoirs from the 1870s on into Edwardian times.

SETTING PLASTER® No.231

A definite pink in historical terms, this color will reward those looking for a solid paint color to reflect the color of plaster. Try using as a wall color with lighter, cool whites.

LOGGIA® No.232

This color matches chips of paint taken from the rendered loggia of a London town house. Presumably painted originally to live with the brickwork.

DAYROOM YELLOW® No.233

So popular throughout the 1980s and 1990s, these sunny yellows actually have their origins in the England of the 1820s. A typical Soanian or Regency color.

VERT DE TERRE® No.234

Reminiscent of the pigment green earth and amusingly to most of us sounding like the French for worm, this is an excellent green. Darker and cooler than the much used No. 32 Cooking Apple Green®, yet lighter and less stony colored than No. 11 Stone White.

BORROWED LIGHT® No.235

There are few Farrow & Ball colors that remain room bound and yet this is probably one of them. A perfect bedroom light blue wall color if not used as a complement to darker colors.

TERESA'S GREEN® No.236

Just lighter in tone than the popular No. 84 Green Blue, this color is also slightly warmer. Though originally found in the eighteenth century, it has been used and reused by successive generations ever since.

COOK'S BLUE® No.237

Reminiscent of Cook's Blue as in the Farrow & Ball book "Paint and Color in Decoration" (pages 180/181). Often found in kitchens and larders during the nineteenth century in the belief that flies never land on it!

MONKEY PUZZLE® No.238

A typical nineteenth-century estate color that has, like so many successful colors, endured down the generations. Good with both brick and stone and indeed furniture.

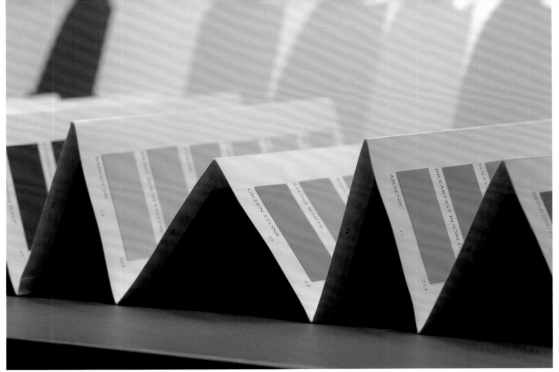

Color cards are hand-painted.

STRONG WHITE® No.2001
Neutral. A bright, clean white when used with dark colors. Or if used with light colors it becomes cool.

WHITE TIE® No.2002
Warm/Neutral. The white of old, pre-brightened, starched cotton.

POINTING® No. 2003
Warm/Neutral. Named after the color of lime pointing used in traditional brickwork.

SLIPPER SATIN® No.2004
Neutral. A very successful off-white for woodwork with strong colors or as a wall color used with many of the other whites, both lighter and darker.

ALL WHITE No.2005
Neutral. Only different-colored white pigments but no modern brighteners used to formulate this bright white.

GREAT WHITE® No.2006
Neutral/Warm. A bright white, but one that is neither "yellow" nor "cold."

DIMITY® No.2008
Warm. Most used as a wall color in its own right with No. 2005 All White or No. 2003 Pointing® on woodwork and ceiling.

CLUNCH® No.2009
Neutral. As in the chalk stone building blocks used in East Anglia. A very versatile off-white.

JAMES WHITE® No.2010
Neutral. A discerning James whose name appears over and over again requesting this lightish broken off-white for use with Farrow & Ball colors.

BLACKENED® No.2011
Neutral/Cool. Simply made with the addition of "lamp black," a pigment made by collecting the residue from burnt lamp oil. To be used as a white with strong colors or as a color of its own with, for example, No. 2005 All White or No. 2003 Pointing®.

HOUSE WHITE® No.2012
Warm. A light yellowed off-white.

MATCHSTICK No.2013
Warm. Mostly used as a warm wall color with lighter cooler woodwork and ceiling whites.

The head-office staff in the paint factory. The total company numbers more than 200 internationally.

GLOSSARY OF FARROW & BALL WALLPAPERS

PAPERS 5
A collection of four designs used in the restoration of great British houses. This block printed collection consists of; "Brockhampton Star," "Garden Trellis" and "Uppark"; "Bumble Bee" is a version of a Napoleonic design found in a French museum.

PAPERS 6
A collection of six designs used in the restoration of great British houses. This block printed collection consists of "5 Over Stripe," "Orleans Stripe," "Ivy," "Four Season Stripe," "Drag" and "Toile Trellis." The feature that coordinates these diverse designs is color.

BLOCK PRINT STRIPES
A collection produced using the traditional block printing method, which enables colors to be printed on top of each other and which imposes infinitely variable patterns on the stripes.

SILVERGATE PAPERS
An early-nineteenth-century damask paper originally printed at Silvergate, a hamlet in Norfolk, England. This is a bold, swirling damask pattern.

ST ANTOINE PAPERS
A stunning Damask collection inspired by a pastoral design created by Réveillon of Paris in 1793. This is a classical French design.

MOUNT ORLEANS PAPERS
Three designs; "Polka Square," "Polka Sprig" and "Sprig Stripe" drawn from background details on eighteenth-century wallpapers found in the Farrow & Ball archives.

PLAIN STRIPES
Inspired by the Farrow & Ball Color Card, these traditional 3-1/2″ self-colored stripes are traditionally "drag" printed with water based paints.

THE DRAGGED PAPERS
Traditionally dragged or strié papers produced using Farrow & Ball colors and water based paints.

TENTED STRIPES
A collection of two types of stripes: the "Tented Stripe," inspired by the Duke of Wellington's campaign tent and the 5-1/4″ "Broad Stripe," sourced from the Farrow & Ball archives.

THE WIMBORNE PAPERS
Inspired by eighteenth-century silk fabric designs, this collection comprises two designs: "St Germain," a breathtaking floral design with bows and tassels, and "Melrose," a smaller and delicately winding pattern. Both designs are traditionally block printed.

VERMICELLI PAPERS
Based on an eighteenth-century Italian textile design, this striking spiral pattern is produced in tone-on-tone colorways and also in striking contemporary silver and gilt colorways.

THE RINGWOLD PAPERS
Originally an English early-eighteenth-century silk, this stylized delicate sprig and berry pattern was originally designed for haute couture clothes.

THE GRISAILLE PAPERS
A stunning collection of 24 designs all printed in a sepia grey colorway to be used in contemporary settings as primary artefacts or as a backdrop to modern or traditional schemes.

SPECIAL BLOCK PRINTS
A special collection of 4 designs: "Gothic" is a faithful reproduction of the rich gothic paper hung in Hanbury Hall, Worcester, England. "Garland" is a nineteenth-century bedroom paper taken from Saltram, in Devon, England; "Sweet Pea" is a classic Edwardian paper; "Beech Leaf" is inspired by an example from the Ironbridge Gorge Museum in England and is typified by a soft elegant shadow.

Stainers, which add the color to the paint, are being poured into pots for mixing.

GLOSSARY OF FARROW & BALL FINISHES

Farrow & Ball paints come in a selection of finishes. Below are their definitions and suggestions for use.

ESTATE® EMULSION

An early highly pigmented formulation that defines the Farrow & Ball look. A durable, matte, softer finish with more depth of colour than other emulsions.

MODERN EMULSION

Completely washable and stain resistant. With a slightly increased sheen level, this wall and ceiling paint is ideal for kitchens, bathrooms and areas of high usage.

OIL EGGSHELL

A low-odor, hard-wearing eggshell finish. Ideal for use on interior woodwork where a low sheen finish is desired, enabling the surface to be easily cleaned. Also suitable for radiators.

WATER BASED EGGSHELL

An environmentally friendly alternative to Oil Eggshell, with excellent flow properties. Like Oil Eggshell, ideal for use on interior woodwork.

DEAD FLAT OIL

Formulated on our fine oil rich resin, this low odor paint has a dead flat finish. For both interior woodwork and plaster where a very matte finish is required.

OIL FULL GLOSS

This low-odor oil paint has a traditional high gloss finish, suitable for both interior and exterior wood and metalwork.

FLOOR PAINT

A very hard-wearing, low-odor, eggshell finish paint for use on interior wood and concrete floors.

EXTERIOR EGGSHELL

A durable, flexible, low-odor eggshell with high resistance to flaking and peeling, for use on softwood or hardwood, including doors, window frames, cladding, barge boards and garden furniture. Also suitable for use on metal surfaces such as railings, gates, guttering and furniture.

The viscosity of the paint is carefully monitored in quality control.

FARROW & BALL'S
NORTH AMERICAN SHOWROOMS

TORONTO
1054 Yonge Street
Toronto, Ontario M4W 2L1
tel 001 416 920 0200

NEW YORK
D&D Building
979 Third Avenue, Suite 1519
New York, NY 10022,
tel 001 212 752 5544

LOS ANGELES
8475 Melrose Avenue,
Los Angeles CA 90069
tel 001 323 655 4499

BOSTON
One Design Center Place, Suite 337A
Boston MA 02210
tel 001 617 345 5344

WASHINGTON
Washington Design Center
300 D Street W, Suite 622,
Washington, DC 20024
tel 001 202 479 6780

GREENWICH
32 East Putnam Avenue
Greenwich CT 06830
tel 203 422 0990

CHICAGO
The Merchandise Mart
222 Merchandise Mart Plaza, Suite 105B
Chicago IL 60654
tel 001 312 222 9620

ACKNOWLEDGMENTS

THE AUTHOR would like to thank the staff at Farrow & Ball, who enthusiastically supported this book from the beginning; the designers and homeowners across the country who welcomed us into their homes; agent Julie Castiglia, who promoted this book from start to finish; and especially publisher Gibbs Smith, who has become an integral part of his life.

THE PHOTOGRAPHER would like to thank the designers and homeowners who opened their hearts and homes to him; Brian Coleman for his sense of humor, which made very long assignments seem like fun weekends; and Michael Tramis, whose technical skills were an asset to the final printed images in this book.